5/85

THE MIXER, BLENDER AND FOOD PROCESSOR COOKBOOK

MARY NORWAK

THE WARWICK PRESS

Acknowledgements

The author and publishers would like to thank
all those who have provided pictures for this
book.
In particular, we would like to thank Moulinex
Limited who have helped with the majority of
photographs.
Additional pictures as follows are the copyright
of Marshall Cavendish Limited: page 22 (photo:
Roger Phillips); page 27 (photo: Alan Duns);
page 38 (photo: Bryce Attwell) and Mrs Julia
Hedgecoe (page 134).

© Mary Norwak 1981
This edition published 1981 by
Ward Lock Limited, 82 Gower Street,
London WC1E 6EQ, a Pentos Company.

Reprinted 1982

Printed and bound in Portugal by Gris Impressores S.A.R.L.

ISBN 0 − 7063 − 4246 − 1

Contents

Notes

Recipes for main meals will serve 4 people.

It is important to follow **either** *the metric* **or** *the imperial measures in any one recipe. Do* **not** *use a combination of metric and imperial.*

All spoon measures are level, and are given in both metric and imperial spoon sizes.

The following symbols are used at the beginning of each recipe method to indicate which appliance to use :

 mixer

 blender

 food processor

Introduction

Ever since primitive man discovered that the application of fire improved the raw foods he had previously eaten, cooks have been working long hours to prepare ingredients. Traditionally, mixtures were creamed with a bare hand, eggs were whisked with twigs or forks, and hard ingredients were chopped with knives.

Simple inventions came slowly to the kitchen, and as late as the end of the eighteenth-century a servant could spend three hours beating a cake mixture. The nineteenth-century saw the development of semi-mechanical whisks, mincers and choppers, but it was not until the middle of the twentieth-century that the electric mixer began to appear on kitchen worktops. It was now possible to mix cakes quickly, rub fat in to make pastry, whip cream and whisk egg whites, thereby eliminating cumbersome tasks and saving endless hours in the kitchen. Soon there were many attachments with devices for chopping, grating and slicing, extracting juice, grinding coffee, sieving purées and making cream.

In the last five years, the food processor has come into our kitchens to tackle nearly all these tasks in one simple machine with few attachments. It is a compact machine designed to stand on a small area of worktop in which many processes may be achieved with one simple knife, although there are one or two attachments for grating and slicing.

These three machines–mixer, blender and food processor–enable the cook to prepare complicated recipes with excellent results; and even simple food preparation will be greatly speeded and improved by their use. The recipes in this book cover a wide range of basic dishes, and alternatives are given for their preparation with each machine, or a combination of them. If you want to adapt any of your own favourite recipes for the machines, follow the general guidelines given in the section on techniques, note the order in which ingredients should be prepared and the way in which they are assembled. Look for a similar recipe in the book which indicates the total weight of ingredients to be processed, and be prepared to halve your own recipe, or to process the ingredients in two or more batches.

Choosing a Machine

A mixer, blender or all-in-one food processor with optional attachments can take the place of a team of cooks. Kitchen tasks such as mincing, chopping, crumbing and creaming become a matter of seconds' work rather than occupying endless arduous hours, and this means that more interesting and complicated recipes can be achieved without worry. These machines also represent a significant saving in money as well as time. Larger batches of food can be processed for freezing or turning into jams or pickles, while leftovers can be transformed into delicious meals, and such oddments as stale bread or ends of cheese can be quickly prepared and will save many pence.

Special recipes are not necessary, but preparation methods and timing do differ from traditional hand-mixing techniques. The recipes in this book will give successful results and, after a little practice, favourite recipes can be adapted to the same techniques outlined here. The blender or processor cut out much preliminary work in recipes, and can also help to cut down actual cooking times in, for instance, the preparation of flour-based sauces.

The larger machines naturally have a wider variety of uses, but when correctly used small machines can also save considerable time, labour and money. The choice of machine naturally depends on price and possible use, as well as the likely space in a kitchen. It may for instance be convenient in a spacious kitchen to have a large mixer with attachments or a food processor, but a smaller kitchen might be better served by a free-standing blender and a hand-held electric mixer, which can be stored easily in a drawer. A single person or small family would be happy with this combination for the making of occasional cakes, for whipping cream or mashing potatoes, preparing individual drinks, and grinding enough coffee for breakfast. A larger family with children might find a larger mixer/blender in constant use for batches of cakes and pastry, puddings and main dishes, and the preparation of drinks and soups. They might also appreciate a mincer attachment to deal with large quantities of raw or cooked meat, or a slicer and shredder for salad preparation. The really keen cook would appreciate a cream-making attachment, juice extractor, or colander-and-sieve for preparing food for the freezer, and a powerful blender for making breadcrumbs, chopping nuts or chocolate.

A food processor can undertake nearly all the combined tasks of both the mixer and blender, and is a useful single machine if space is limited.

Types of machine

A large mixer with a stand and bowl is often available with a variety of attachments. It is strong enough to tackle up to quite large quantities, provided they are added in small amounts. These machines are heavy and must be kept permanently in a convenient place, to be used at the turn of a switch.

A small mixer may be with or without a stand and bowl. It is less powerful and must not be overstrained, so it should not be used for heavy mixtures or large quantities. Some small mixers are attached to their stands; others can be detached and used as hand-held mixers. A hand-held mixer is often a useful supplement to a larger one for a busy cook, for whipping cream or egg whites. Hand-held mixers are mainly designed for whisking, but can also be used for light creaming and 'rubbing-in'. Care must be taken not to overstrain the motor with heavy work. Some of these mixers have only a single speed. Others, however, have variable speeds to suit the work involved.

A small blender may be free-standing or an attachment. It is useful for all blending jobs, plus really fine chopping and grinding. Some free-standing models have special grinder attachments for this work. This type of blender should be run for a few seconds only at a time to avoid overheating, and it should not be used for very stiff mixtures. Food can only be blended in small quantities, so soups and drinks may be laborious and messy to make. More liquid may be needed in more powerful blenders, and this may limit one in making highly spiced mixtures.

A large blender may also be either free-standing or an attachment to a mixer. It normally has a working capacity of 900ml/ 1½ pints or over. This type of blender can tackle all kinds of blending jobs, and can often be used additionally for chopping or grinding.

A wide-based blender is powerful and not suitable for small quantities of ingredients or for fine chopping; it purées them too soon. However, this type is particularly good for large amounts of drinks or soups, and can also be used for such jobs as rubbing fat into flour.

A blender is a useful maid-of-all work, but there are one or two jobs better handled by other tools. A blender cannot be used for beating egg whites or for crushing whole ice cubes (cubes have to be broken into small pieces before adding to liquids in the blender). It cannot be used for mashing potatoes, processing large quantities of cooked meat, or mincing raw meat, and it will not slice or shave nuts. Although it can be used for making cake batters and for quick creaming of fat, eggs and sugar, it is not suitable for making a complete cake mixture, which is better finished off with a mixer beater. It also cannot be used for mixing light sponge cakes.

A food processor has a powerful motor base fitted with a cylindrical container and a variety of knives and shredding discs. Jobs are done according to the knife or shredder which is attached, and the motor is controlled by movement of the bowl or a button. Many food processors only have one speed, but some have two speeds controlled by the knife or attachment which is used.

Mixer Attachments and What They Do

Additional attachments that can be speedily fitted to large mixers are available. They do many specialized jobs and are very useful when large quantities of food have to be prepared, or if certain routine tasks occur frequently, such as the extraction of fruit juice or the preparation of yeast doughs. Full instructions for fitting and use are given with each attachment, but a brief indication of their various uses will enable a mixer-owner to ascertain if they are necessary.

Bean Slicer and Pea Huller
The bean slicing attachment can also be converted to use for shelling peas. This is a useful machine if a large quantity of garden produce is to be processed for home freezing.

Can Opener
This attachment opens any shape of can speedily and efficiently, with no danger of cut fingers. A magnet lifts the lid clear.

Coffee Mill
This attachment grinds coffee beans to the degree required from coarse to fine. Many people will find a blender adequate to grind coffee.

Colander-and-Sieve
This attachment is useful for preparing purées and baby foods. While a blender or food processor will purée cooked or raw ingredients, it is necessary to sieve such items as gooseberries and currants to remove the pips. The colander and sieve are also useful for converting garden produce for bottling or home freezing.

Cream Maker
This attachment is used to make thick or pouring cream from unsalted butter and warm milk, and it can also be used for ice cream preparation.

Dough Hook
This hook is used for kneading yeast doughs, and makes light work of this rather heavy task. As this is a very inexpensive attachment, it is well worth buying for anyone who likes to make bread or yeast cakes.

Juice Extractor
This attachment extracts all juice from oranges, lemons or grapefruit. It is very useful for mothers of small children. With the addition of an *oil dripper*, it can be used to make mayonnaise, although this can be made equally well by the mixer beaters or blender.

Juice Separator
This attachment is used to extract juice from fruit or vegetables, straining it at the same time, and will tackle 450g/1lb of fruit or vegetables at a time. It consists of a drum container fitted with a plastic filter and straining basket which is attached to the high-speed outlet of a mixer.

Mincer and Sausage Filler
The mincer has both fine and large-hole mincing screens, so that mixtures may be cut finely for pies and pâtés, or coarsely for sausages or animal food. The mincer includes a pestle for pushing food down into the machine, which can deal speedily with large quantities of meat, fish and vegetables. An inexpensive sausage filler can be fitted to the mincer to enable the minced meat to be fed into sausage skins.

Potato Peeler
This attachment can be used to peel any root vegetable very cleanly, and is useful when large quantities are required.

Slicer and Shredder
This attachment consists of four 'drums', which produce slices or shreds of such foods as root vegetables, apples, cabbages, onions, potatoes, cheese, suet, nuts, chocolate and cucumber. It is useful for anyone who makes large quantities of salads. It doubles up as a grater.

Food Processor Attachments and What They Do

Blender Attachment
Available with a few models, the blender attachment handles larger quantities of liquid ingredients than the basic food processor.

Cutting Discs
A wide range of cutting, shredding, grating and slicing attachments is available, according to model, for preparing vegetables and salads, chipping potatoes, and grating hard cheese and chocolate.

Juice Extractor
This extracts juice from oranges, lemons and grapefruit, and is useful if large quantities are to be prepared. It is available on a few models only.

Metal Blade
All food processors are fitted with a metal blade which can be used for chopping and mixing, preparing breadcrumbs, creaming cakes and making batters and purées. It will also crush ice. The blade is strong enough to chop raw meat, vegetables, fruit, etc, without the addition of liquid.

Plastic Blade
Some food processors have an additional plastic blade which is used for making pastry and rubbed-in and one-stage creamed cakes. The blade will also smooth sauces, and prepare small quantities of bread dough. In some machines, this plastic blade selects a lower speed for these processes. The metal blade can be substituted for most recipes, according to the model chosen. If in doubt, refer to the manufacturer's instructions.

Whisk Attachment
This is available in a few models for whisking egg whites and whipping cream.

Basic Techniques and Maintenance

It is most important that all machines are kept on a working surface where they can be used regularly as part of kitchen routine. If they are put away in cupboards, or high on shelves, it will be an effort to make use of them, and their potential for saving time and energy will be minimized. If the machine is ready set up, it can be used dozens of times in the course of a cooking session, quickly washed and reassembled and the cook will speed up her routine and produce far more and far better dishes.

It is best to process small quantities of food at a time, and to switch on and off once or twice during working time. Often, it is necessary to scrape down food in mixing bowls or blender goblets. This should never be done while the motor is running, and sharp implements such as knives or spoons should not be used; most machines are supplied with a suitable spatula. Always disconnect machines when not in use.

Basic Mixer Technique

Hand-made recipes can be used for an electric mixer without difficulty, but it is very easy to work the machine too quickly or for too long and an over-beaten mixture will spoil results. Start mixtures on slow speed, and increase speed as required, but don't leave the machine to work away on its own without constant checks to see that the mixture is not being overworked since this

can damage the machine. A mixer should, in principle, not run for more than 3 minutes at a time.

Some mixers have planetary action with the beaters turning and revolving on axis, so that the mixture comes cleanly from the sides of the bowl, and mixing is more thorough and smoother. Ordinary beaters force the mixture outwards so that it clings to the sides of the mixing bowl. If the mixture adheres to the sides of the bowl, stop the machine and scrape down the sides with a spatula or wooden spoon before starting the motor again. For the best results, ingredients should be at room temperature, as mixing will take longer if the ingredients are cold.

Running Speeds (mixer)

The correct speed for a mixer can be judged by the work to be done and the quantity of ingredients involved. Basically, a heavy mixture needs slow beating, and over-beating will result in heavy cakes, grainy cream and curdled eggs. For a light mixture, a higher speed is needed.

Use a *low speed* for rubbing in pastry and cakes, *medium speed* for creaming mixtures, and *high speed* for whisking egg whites. The heavy beater of a large mixer is generally used for cake mixtures and the whisk for light egg whites or very light mixtures. When a mixer has a variety of speeds, the speed may be altered during processing.

Often a recipe recommends starting on a low speed, and then increasing speed for final mixing once the ingredients have been incorporated.

Quantities (mixer)

While the mixer is useful for making two cakes at a time and saves a lot of effort, it is important not to over-fill the bowl. Recommended quantities for a large mixer are:

Egg whites

10-12 (300ml/$\frac{1}{2}$ pint) maximum; 1 egg white minimum.

Cake or pudding mixture

2·7kg/6lb all ingredients maximum; 50g/2oz butter with 50g/2oz sugar minimum.

Pastry

675g/1$\frac{1}{2}$lb flour and 350g/12oz fat maximum; 100g/4oz flour and 50g/2oz fat minimum.

Yeast dough

900g/2lb flour and proportionate ingredients.

Basic Blender Technique

A blender works by forming a vortex or 'hole' in the mixture. Briefly, the mixture to be blended is pushed up the sides of the goblet and then falls down into the centre and on to the blades. To prevent the blender labouring too hard, start with a small amount of the liquid used in the recipe. Cut fruit, vegetables and meat into small cubes, and break bread or biscuits into small chunks. Remove any fruit stones, or pieces of bones from meat before blending. Use a low speed for chopping and for coarse textures, and start at a low speed increasing to high when larger quantities of food are being blended (over half a goblet full). Work in only small quantities of heavy mixture at a time, and switch quickly 'off' then 'on' to low or high speed to push the food down on to the blades to avoid damaging the machine. Generally, a blender should not run for more than 45-60 seconds at a time. If food gets lodged under the blades, stop the machine and scrape the blades with a rubber or plastic spatula or wooden spoon. Scrape or push the food down from time to time, but don't do this while the motor is running.

It is important never to over-fill the goblet, and to cover it before blending. Hold the lid lightly in place with one hand when starting the motor. The lid should not be taken off during use, unless extra ingredients have to be added while the machine is running, but this is best done by removing the central knob in the lid.

When using a blender recipe, add the ingredients to the goblet in the order given. If you are adapting a normal recipe, try to adapt to blender technique by blending liquids or soft ingredients first, adding ingredients to be chopped or ground after the first blending. See that fats and eggs are at room temperature, or melt the fat before blending. Liquids may be warmed before adding to ease blending, but hot liquids should not be put in the goblet. Be careful not to overblend, since this will spoil the texture of food. Time the blending, using correct speeds, and watch the consistency of food being blended. When chopping such items as nuts, only process a small quantity at a time, or the nuts lower in the goblet will be ground to a fine powder by the time the nuts above are chopped. Follow manufacturers' instructions very carefully if grinding hard substances such as coffee beans, chocolate or nuts, or if preparing raw meat or fish. As with mixers, it is important not to over-process ingredients and to time processing carefully at the correct speed for the job.

A blender motor is dangerously powerful, and children should be kept away from the blender when it is in use. See that nobody puts fingers, hands or implements into the goblet while the motor is running. Do see that it is always firmly attached to the base when running, and standing firmly on a level surface.

Running Speeds (blender)

Some blenders have a marked dial, or a series of buttons, either marked 'off', 'low' and 'high', or with a set of numbers. High speed or a high number is for liquid mixtures, while low speed or low numbers are for mixing heavier ingredients, or for chopping.

Quantities (blender)

A blender should never be filled more than three-quarters full, and it is wise to divide recipe quantities into small amounts if necessary. Workable blending quantities are:

Liquids
600ml/1 pint to 900ml/1½ pints, according to size of blender.

Pastes and spreads
100g/4oz at one time.

Bread and biscuit crumbs
50g/2oz at one time.

Cooked vegetables for purée
100g/4oz at one time.

Soups
600ml/1 pint liquid and 225g/8oz solids.

Fruit for purée
50g/2oz at one time, without pips or stones.

Dried fruit
50g/2oz at one time.

Batter
600ml/1 pint.

Basic Food Processor Technique

Follow the manufacturer's instruction book when first assembling the machine. Be sure that the bowl sits firmly on the drive shaft, and then insert the required blade or other attachment before putting food into the bowl. If a blade is used, put in the ingredients and put on the cover before activating the motor with a button or by twisting the cover (according to model). The cover cannot be removed while the machine is in operation. Be careful, however, to use the pusher when pushing ingredients through the feeder tube so that fingers, knives or spoons do not come into contact with the cutting discs. Always remove the work bowl from the motor base when taking out blades or attachments so that liquid does not spill through the centre of the bowl and accumulate round the drive shaft.

Like the mixer and blender, the food processor performs at its best in a series of very short operations. As it operates very quickly, care must be taken that ingredients are not over-processed. The machine must be stopped instantly when the required results are achieved. It is a good idea before starting a recipe to look carefully through the list of ingredients. Sometimes you may find that you can chop all the dry ingredients first to save washing the bowl each time. Do not overload the machine; it is best not to process more than 450g/1lb food at a time. Be prepared to process two or three batches of ingredients, and remember to cut food to be chopped into cubes not larger than 2·5cm/ 1in. Do not chop frozen or unboned meat.

Keep the metal blade, cutting attachments and any other pieces of equipment in a cupboard or rack above the machine, safely out of the reach of children.

Maintenance of Mixers, Blenders and Food Processors

To wash a mixer beater, bowl, blender goblet or other attachment, put into warm soapy water, rinse and dry thoroughly. If food particles are lodged under the blades of a blender, put some warm water and liquid detergent into the blender goblet and run the machine very briefly before rinsing and drying. All metal parts of a machine or its attachments should be washed in warm soapy water (not washing soda), then dried well before storage. All plastic parts should be wiped over with hot soapy water and well dried, but not exposed to direct heat such as a cooker or oven. Wash glass parts with hot soapy water, but do not expose them to sudden changes of temperature. Wipe the motor base with a damp cloth and dry well. Do not immerse in water.

Attachments used for preparing fruit, vegetables or fruits which stain should also be washed straight after use. These must be dried very carefully, and stored loosely assembled so that air can circulate.

Failures and Remedies

There is an obvious difference between hand and machine techniques, which can create small problems during machine preparation, or poor textured results when the cook first uses a mixer, blender or food processor. Experience in use usually overcomes these difficulties, but it is possible to avoid problems right from the beginning. The following points indicate the problems and their remedies.

Mixture sticks to bowl or beater
(mixer)
This indicates that the ingredients are not warm enough. Fat should always be at room temperature before being used. Eggs which have been stored in a refrigerator or very cold place should also be at room temperature before being used.

Mixture climbs too high up sides of bowl (mixer)
This means that the mixer is being used at too high a speed. The motor should be stopped and the mixture scraped back into the bottom of the bowl before the motor is switched on again at a lower speed.

Small quantity of mixture is not mixed thoroughly (mixer)
The beater may need closer adjustment to the bowl of the mixer.

Egg whites are not whisked high and fluffy (mixer, food processor)
This can mean that the eggs are too new, or too cold. It may also indicate that the speed is too slow. It is also important that the bowl and whisk should be completely clean and dry, and free from egg yolk or grease. The whisk should be adjusted as closely as possible, and the maximum speed should be used.

Pastry is 'short' and difficult to roll
(mixer, food processor)
This can mean that too much fat has been used, or that it has been overmixed. A mixer rubs in very thoroughly, so that a little less fat can be used than usual, and the work is done in a very short time. When liquid is added, it should also be put in quickly and the motor turned off as soon as it has been incorporated, or the pastry will be over-mixed. When using a food processor, the fat will also be rubbed in quickly. Add the water, and only process until a ball of dough is formed, switching off immediately.

Pastry is like rubber
(mixer, food processor)
Water has been added too slowly and mixed in between additions. Water should be tipped into the pastry quickly and the machine switched off at once.

Cake is 'heavy' (mixer, food processor)
This indicates that the flour has been mixed in too vigorously, or for too long. With a mixer, flour should be folded in at minimum speed, and the machine should be

switched off as soon as it is incorporated. With a food processor, only process until the flour has just been absorbed.

Food is chopped too finely
(blender, food processor)
With a blender or food processor, it is very easy to over-chop so that items such as nuts are ground finely instead of being chopped. Only process small quantities at a time. Work on minimum speed for a very short time.

Food sticks and is not blended
(blender, food processor)
This indicates that there is not enough liquid in a blender goblet, or that a blender or food processor is overloaded. When using a food processor, check quantities of ingredients carefully as the capacity of the machine is limited. When using a blender, solid ingredients should be added slowly in small quantities so that blending is smooth and even. If the mixture sticks, stop the motor and scrape down the sides, or remove some of the ingredients and process smaller quantities. In a creamed mixture, the ingredients may be too cold.

Cream curdles (blender, food processor)
This means that cream has been over-mixed in a blender or food processor. It should be added gradually, and the machine switched off as soon as the cream has been mixed in.

Cheese packs together
(blender, food processor)
Oil is pressed out from some cheeses during blending or processing, and it is a good idea to put a little flour or bread from a recipe into the machine with the cheese during processing so that it absorbs the oil and enables the cheese to grate evenly.

Cheese sauce curdles (mixer, blender, food processor)
This will happen if the raw cheese is blended with the other raw ingredients before cooking, and it will overcook. Grate the cheese separately and add to the cooked sauce.

Icing is too soft
(blender, food processor)
Ingredients in a blender or food processor should be at room temperature; if they are too warm, processing will thin the mixture. Leave the icing to firm up before using.

Saving Time and Money

It is obvious that the mixer, blender, food processor and attachments save a great deal of time in the preparation of recipes. They can also save considerable time in preparing useful ingredients, such as chopping nuts, grating cheese or making breadcrumbs. This in turn can save money, when leftovers such as cheese and bread are processed and stored for later use in recipes. The blender is useful for converting leftovers into economical soups and pastes, and the food processor may be used in the same way. There is also great advantage to the keen cook, in being able to prepare flavoured butters, marzipan, praline and jam glazes quickly and cheaply, while the busy cook will be glad to be able to prepare baby food, invalid diets or health food herself, saving not only money but shopping time.

Biscuits and Cake Crumbs

Blend broken sweet biscuits on medium speed to make coarse or fine crumbs for flan cases, cheesecake bases, or uncooked biscuit-cakes. Cake crumbs may be blended to use in puddings. The food processor will make crumbs easily, using the metal blade.

Breadcrumbs

Crumbs can vary from rough to powder texture, according to their intended use. Fresh bread should be processed in very small amounts. Stale bread will 'crumb' more easily, and bread can be crisped in the oven before blending to make crisp crumbs for coating food.

Break bread into pieces about 2·5cm/1in square. Blend a little at a time, stopping the machine to scrape down, and empty out crumbs as they are made. A food processor makes crumbs in larger quantities without the necessity of scraping down.

Butter (mixer)

About 600ml/1 pint cream is the smallest practical quantity to use, and it should be four days old. Put into the mixing bowl, and mix on low speed using the heavy beater. Continue beating until the butter comes into one lump. Switch off the motor and drain the buttermilk to use for cooking. Wash the butter in cold water until the water remains clear. Squeeze to extract the water, add salt to taste and pat the butter into shape.

Butter (blender)

Blend cream on *high* speed for about 1 minute. Drain off the buttermilk to use for cooking. Put clean cold water into the blender with the cream. Blend for 10 seconds, pour away the water, and squeeze the butter to extract the water. Add salt to taste, and pat the butter into shape.

Candied Peel

Candied peel should be cut into 2·5cm/1in pieces, and fed gradually into the blender. Not more than 75g/3oz should be processed at one time. It is a good idea to blend the peel with a little icing sugar to prevent stickiness. Peel may also be chopped to the required fineness with the metal blade of food processor.

Cheese

Cut cheese into 2·5cm/1in cubes and feed gradually into the blender. Very hard cheese such as Parmesan should be cut into smaller pieces. As soon as the cheese becomes sticky, switch off, empty out the cheese, and process another quantity. About 50g/2oz cheese should be processed in each batch. High speed for 6 seconds should be enough to grate most cheeses. Cheese may also be chopped coarsely or finely with the metal blade of a food processor. A grating attachment to a mixer or food processor will produce a finer result.

Children's Food

Food suitable for children can be blended, or smoothed with the plastic blade of a food processor. A coarser texture can be produced for slightly older children. This means that meat, fish, poultry and vegetables from the ordinary family meal can be utilized; fruit and custard or milk puddings or cereal can be blended for a sweet course.

Dried milk for babies can be smoothly prepared in a blender which has been washed, rinsed and scalded before use. Powdered cereals can also be added to the milk in the blender. Flavoured milk drinks, or combinations of milk and eggs, or milk and fruit, will be popular with older children. A food processor is not suitable.

Chocolate

Block chocolate should be broken up in small pieces and processed in a blender at low speed to the required fineness. Not more than 75g/3oz should be chopped or grated at one time. Chocolate may be chopped with the metal blade of a food processor, or grated with a grating attachment.

Coffee

A grinding attachment may be used on a mixer to grind coffee beans. If using a blender, put in just enough coffee beans to cover the knives, or fill not more than one-third full, timing to give a coarse or fine grind. Use the metal blade of a food processor to grind to the required fineness.

Cream

Cream may be whipped by the blender, but will have greater volume if prepared with a mixer. Timing must be carefully watched and the blender must be stopped immediately the cream is thick. Keep turning the blender off and on rather than blending continuously. A food processor cannot be used to whip cream unless it has a whisking attachment.

Diet Foods

For bland diets, or where an individual has to be fed, the blender can be used to make solid food into purée. A colander-and-sieve attachment for a mixer is also useful for this type of food, and a food processor may also be used. Juicy fruits or vegetables require little or no extra liquid, but meat and fish can be made into a purée with milk, water, stock or egg. When using a blender, it should be started on *low* speed, and if the purée is thick, it should be scraped down from the sides of the blender with the motor turned off before continuing processing.

Dried Milk

Milk will be smooth if the water is put into a blender goblet before the dried milk powder. Blend together at maximum speed for a few seconds. Dried milk may be prepared in the same way in a food processor, but only in small quantities.

Fruit Juices

Canned and frozen juices taste fresh and delicious if blended for a few seconds at high speed, switching on and off once or twice during blending. Crushed ice can be added to the juices during blending. If using a food processor with a plastic blade, only blend up to 300ml/$\frac{1}{2}$ pint liquid.

Health Foods

A blender can be used to retain the complete goodness of fruit and vegetables for soups and drinks. Yoghurt can be blended into drinks, and wheatgerm added for extra nourishment. If a juice-separator attachment is available, additional fruit and vegetable juices and extracts of herbs can be processed. Those who wish to avoid flour or fats will find that sauces and soups can, with the aid of a blender, be made without thickening. A food processor may be used in the same way, but only fill the bowl one-third full.

Herbs

Chop herbs in a blender by dropping sprigs of fresh herbs on to the cutters as they rotate. A little liquid aids easy blending. With a food processor, use the metal blade and put in as many sprigs of herbs as needed before processing, without liquid.

Ice

Wrap ice in a cloth and break roughly with a hammer. Put into a blender or food processor for crushing, and empty out as soon as broken up as ice will liquefy quickly.

Jams and Marmalade

The blender can chop such fruit as rhubarb, dried apricots and oranges for preserving, using the water to be included in the recipe, and this will greatly speed up the cooking time. A food processor may be used for this chopping, but no liquid will be needed.

Jam Glaze

A smooth jam glaze can be blended to use as a finish for flans, etc. Melt 100g/4oz apricot, strawberry or raspberry jam, or redcurrant jelly with 150ml/$\frac{1}{4}$ pint water. Boil for 4 minutes. Put into the blender with 5ml/1 teaspoon lemon juice and blend until smooth; sieve if necessary to remove pips. A food processor with a plastic blade may be used instead.

Leftovers

All kinds of leftover food can be used for a second meal after blending. Leftover meat, poultry or fish can be coarsely ground for use in loaves, mousses, soufflés and galantines. Small quantities of the same food can be blended into spreads and pastes. Vegetables, stock and gravy can be blended into soups. Fruit can be made into a purée to blend into soups. Fruit can be made into a purée to blend with cream as a food, or can be blended with custard or milk pudding to make a whip. Bread, biscuits, cakes and cheese can all be blended to use as toppings, or as part of complete recipes. A food processor may be used in the same way as a blender to deal with leftovers.

Marzipan

A mixer can be used to make fine-texture marzipan very quickly. Mix 175g/6oz caster sugar and 175g/6oz icing sugar in the bowl with 350g/12oz ground almonds. Using the heavy beater at minimum speed, mix for 10 seconds. Add 1 egg and 10ml/2 teaspoons each of lemon juice and brandy, and increase the speed slightly until a smooth paste is formed, being careful not to overmix as the marzipan will become oily. A food processor with a plastic blade may be used instead, adding the liquid through the feeder tube with the machine running.

Nuts

Blend a few nuts at a time, turning on and off at *low* speed until chopped to the required fineness. If using the metal blade of a food processor chop nuts coarsely or finely.

Pastry and Scone Mixes

To save time, make up large batches of pastry and scone mixes with the heavy beater on a mixer or with the plastic blade of a food processor. Use flour and fat, but do not add water. Store the 'crumb' mixture in a polythene bag in a refrigerator. Weigh out when required and complete with milk or water as necessary.

Praline

Home-made praline is very useful for flavouring and decorating soufflés, creams and ices. Put together 75g/3oz caster sugar and 75g/3oz whole unblanched almonds in a thick saucepan, and set over low heat. Do not stir until the sugar has melted and is turning in colour. Stir frequently until a rich caramel colour, with the almonds well toasted. Turn on to an oiled tin. When hard, break into pieces and blend on *low* speed, or with the metal blade of a food processor, until powdery. Keep in an airtight tin.

If preferred, nut brittle may be bought and processed in the same way.

Pulses and Rice

Lentils, split peas, rice, etc can be treated like coffee beans, and this cuts down cooking time if they are finely ground for soups.

Purées

Soft raw vegetables and fruit such as tomatoes and strawberries, or cooked fruit or vegetables, need no extra liquid to become purée. They may be put through the colander-and-sieve attachment of a mixer, or blended on *high* speed and sieved if necessary. The goblet should only be half-full, and fruit need not be peeled before converting it into purée. A food processor may be used to make purée, but should only be filled one-third full. The metal blade may be needed first to chop raw fruit and vegetables finely and the plastic blade will smooth out the mixture.

Sugar

Granulated sugar may be refined in a food processor, or by blending at maximum speed for 30 seconds to produce caster sugar. Do not fill the processor or blender goblet more than a quarter full. Caster sugar may be reduced to a powder to use as icing sugar, but will be slightly gritty and greyish in colour. Coloured sugar can be made for cakes and puddings if a few drops of food colouring are added during processing. The sugar should be stirred with a spatula once during blending to distribute colour.

Soups

Artichoke Soup

675g/1½lb Jerusalem
    artichokes
5ml/1 teaspoon lemon juice
1 small onion
50g/2oz butter
900ml/1½ pints stock
15g/½oz cornflour
75ml/3fl oz single cream
salt and pepper

Peel and slice the artichokes and put them into a little water with the lemon juice to prevent discoloration. Skin the onion and chop it coarsely in the blender. Melt the butter and cook the chopped onion gently in it until soft but not brown. Add the artichoke slices and continue cooking for 5 minutes. Put the artichokes, onions and liquid from the cooking into the blender, with the stock. Add the cornflour mixed with a little cold stock. Blend for 1 minute until smooth. Re-heat and stir in the cream just before serving. Season with salt and pepper to taste. Be careful not to boil the soup when the cream has been added.

Make as above, but slice the artichokes with the slicing disc and chop the onions with the metal blade. If a blender is not available, process the artichokes and onions without liquid until smooth, using the metal blade, then return to the saucepan.

Asparagus Soup

1 small onion
50g/2oz butter
25g/1oz plain flour
350g/12oz cooked or canned
    asparagus
600ml/1 pint chicken stock
300ml/½ pint milk
salt and pepper

Skin the onion and chop it coarsely in the blender. Melt the butter, and cook the onion until soft but not brown. Work in the flour, and continue cooking, stirring well, for 1 minute. Put the mixture into the blender with the asparagus cut in pieces, add stock and milk. Blend for 1 minute. Simmer gently for 5 minutes, and season to taste with salt and pepper. A few asparagus tips may be reserved for garnish.

Make as above, but chop the onions with the metal blade. Process the cooked onion and asparagus until smooth, using the metal blade, then add the liquid.

Celery Soup

10 sticks celery
1 medium onion
900ml/1½ pints chicken stock
5ml/1 teaspoon salt

Cut the celery into 2·5cm/1in pieces. Skin the onion and cut  into pieces. Put the celery, onion and stock into the blender, and chop coarsely. It may be necessary to process the vegetables in two or three lots so that the blender is not overloaded. Put into a saucepan with the salt, bring to the boil, and then simmer for 10 minutes. Put into the blender and blend until smooth. Re-heat and serve hot with cubes of fried bread.

If a cream soup is preferred, use 300ml/½ pint creamy milk instead of part of the stock, and add it at the second blending stage.

Make as above, but chop the celery and onion with the metal blade. Process the cooked onion and celery with a little stock until smooth, using the metal blade, then return to the saucepan with the remaining liquid.

Chilled Beetroot Soup

450g/1lb cooked beetroot
900ml/1½ pints water
2 small lemons
3 size 3-4 eggs
5ml/1 teaspoon salt
15ml/1 tablespoon liquid
  honey

Peel the beetroot and cut into pieces. Put into the blender with water and blend until finely chopped. Put into a saucepan and bring to the boil. Meanwhile, peel the lemons and remove the pips. Cut the flesh into pieces and blend until smooth. Add to the beetroot, and simmer for 15 minutes. Take off the heat and cool for 10 minutes. In a bowl, mix the eggs, salt and honey, and gradually pour in the beetroot mixture. Stir well and serve cold. If liked, the soup can be returned to the blender when the eggs have been added, and blended until completely smooth.

Make as above, but chop the beetroot with the metal blade before putting it in the pan with water. Chop the lemons and process until smooth with the metal blade, then add to the beetroot. Return to the processor, if liked, and blend until smooth, using the metal blade.

Asparagus Soup

Cod Chowder

675g/1½lb cod (or haddock)
600ml/1 pint water
1 large onion
50g/2oz butter
2 large potatoes
3 celery sticks
25g/1oz plain flour
1·5 litres/2½ pints milk
15ml/1 tablespoon
   Worcestershire sauce
salt and pepper
1 sprig of parsley

Cover the fish with the water and simmer for 20 minutes.
Drain, retaining the cooking liquid. Remove the skin and
bones, and flake the fish with a fork. Skin the onion and
chop it finely (metal blade). Melt the butter in a pan and
cook the onion over low heat for 5 minutes until soft and
golden. Peel the potatoes and wash and trim the celery. Chop
the potatoes and celery coarsely (metal blade). Add to the
onions and stir over low heat for 5 minutes. Stir in the flour
and cook for 1 minute. Gradually work in the milk and then
add the flaked fish and half the reserved cooking liquid.
Bring to the boil and then simmer for 15 minutes. Season
with Worcestershire sauce, salt and pepper, and simmer for
5 minutes. Chop the parsley (metal blade) and sprinkle over
the chowder before serving.

Make as above, but chop the onion, potatoes and celery in a
blender, adding a little cooking liquid, if necessary.

Country Carrot Soup

675g/1½lb carrots
450g/1lb potatoes
225g/8oz onions
75g/3oz butter
1·2 litres/2 pints chicken stock
salt and pepper
1 bay leaf
1 sprig of thyme
3 sprigs parsley

Peel the carrots, potatoes and onions. Slice the carrots with
the slicing attachment of a mixer, or chop in a blender.
Quarter the potatoes and onions and chop them in a blender,
adding a little stock if necessary. Melt the butter in a heavy-
based pan and cook the onions gently for 5 minutes, stirring
well. Add the carrots and potatoes, and continue cooking for
10 minutes, stirring often. Add the stock, salt, pepper, bay
leaf, thyme and 1 sprig of parsley. Bring to the boil, and then
cover and simmer for 25 minutes until the vegetables are
soft. Remove the bay leaf, thyme and parsley. Strain the
liquid into a clean pan. Blend the vegetables until smooth
and creamy, adding a little cooking liquid if necessary. Add
to the liquid in the pan and re-heat gently. Chop the remaining parsley and sprinkle over the soup just before serving.
If liked, serve with small cubes of toasted or fried bread.

Make as above, but use the slicing disc for the carrots. Chop
the potatoes and onions using the metal blade.

Cream of Mushroom Soup

1 small onion
1 streaky bacon rasher,
    without rinds
225g/8oz mushrooms
25g/1oz butter
25g/1oz plain flour
600ml/1 pint chicken stock
300ml/½ pint milk
salt and pepper
150ml/¼ pint single cream
6 stems chives

Skin the onion and chop it finely (metal blade). Chop the
bacon coarsely (metal blade). Wipe the mushrooms and slice
(slicing disc). Melt the butter in a pan and cook the onion
and bacon over low heat, stirring well, for 5 minutes. Add
the mushrooms and stir over low heat for 5 minutes. Stir in
the flour and cook for 2 minutes. Add the stock and milk,
stir well and bring to the boil. Season with salt and pepper,
cover and simmer for 20 minutes. Cool slightly and blend
until smooth. Stir in the cream and heat very gently but do
not boil. Chop the chives (metal blade) and sprinkle over the
soup.

Make as above, but chop the onion and bacon in a blender.
Slice the mushrooms with the slicing attachment of a mixer
or chop in a blender.

Cream of Green Pea Soup

450g/1lb fresh or frozen green
    peas
1 small onion
50g/2oz butter
1 sprig of parsley
5ml/1 teaspoon salt
5ml/1 teaspoon sugar
a pinch of pepper
a pinch of ground nutmeg
300ml/½ pint water
300ml/½ pint milk
150ml/¼ pint single cream
1 sprig of mint

If using frozen peas, allow them to thaw until just softened
before using. Skin the onion and chop it finely (metal blade).
Melt the butter in a pan and cook the onion over low heat,
stirring well, for 5 minutes. Add the peas, parsley, salt, sugar,
pepper, nutmeg and water. Cover and simmer for 20 minutes. Cool slightly and blend until smooth. Add the milk and
blend until mixed. Return to the saucepan and re-heat
gently. Sir in the cream and re-heat gently without boiling.
Chop the mint (metal blade) and use to garnish the soup.

Make as above, but chop the onion in a blender.

Creamed Fish Soup

1 small onion
350g/12oz white fish
300ml/½ pint water
25g/1oz butter
15ml/1 tablespoon parsley
25g/1oz plain flour
300ml/½ pint milk
salt and pepper
50g/2oz peeled shrimps

Skin and chop the onion and put into the water with the fish.
Simmer until just soft. Put into the blender, including the
cooking liquid, with the butter, parsley, flour and milk.
Blend until smooth. Pour into a saucepan and heat gently,
stirring until smooth and hot. Season to taste and garnish
with shrimps.

Note The fish can be a mixture of white fish; a little smoked
haddock may be included.

Make as above, but chop the onion with the metal blade.
Process the cooked onion and fish with a little cooking liquid,
butter, parsley and flour using the metal blade, then add to
the remaining cooking liquid and milk in the saucepan.

Fresh Tomato Soup

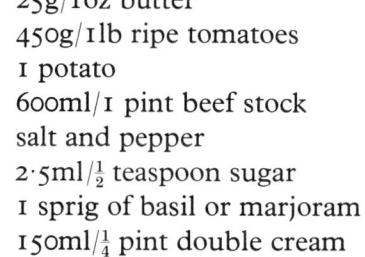

1 small onion
1 bacon rasher, without rinds
25g/1oz butter
450g/1lb ripe tomatoes
1 potato
600ml/1 pint beef stock
salt and pepper
2·5ml/½ teaspoon sugar
1 sprig of basil or marjoram
150ml/¼ pint double cream
5ml/1 teaspoon grated orange
    rind

Skin the onion and chop it finely (metal blade). Chop the
bacon coarsely (metal blade). Melt the butter in a pan and
stir the onion and bacon over low heat for 5 minutes. Skin
the tomatoes by dipping them in boiling water. Cut them
in quarters and discard the pips. Chop the flesh coarsely
(metal blade) and add to the onion mixture. Cook gently for
5 minutes. Peel the potato and cut in pieces. Chop coarsely
(metal blade) and add to the tomatoes. Add the stock, salt,
pepper, sugar and sprig of basil or marjoram. Bring to the
boil, then cover and simmer for 30 minutes. Cool slightly and
blend until smooth. Re-heat gently. Just before serving,
whip the cream to soft peaks. Pour the soup into individual
bowls and garnish each with a spoonful of cream sprinkled
with a little grated orange rind.

Make as above, but chop the onion, bacon, tomato flesh and
potato in a blender. Use the whisk attachment of a mixer, if
available, to whip the cream.

Florentine Soup

900g/2lb fresh spinach
100g/4oz onions
50g/2oz butter
900ml/1½ pints chicken stock
salt and pepper
a pinch of ground nutmeg
60ml/4 tablespoons single
    cream
50g/2oz Cheddar cheese

Remove the stems from the spinach and wash the leaves thoroughly. Put into a large saucepan and just cover with boiling water. Bring to the boil quickly and drain thoroughly. Cool completely under running water. Skin the onions and chop finely in a blender. Melt the butter and stir the onions over low heat for 5 minutes until soft and golden. Drain the spinach thoroughly and add to the pan. Stir well to coat with butter, cover and simmer for 10 minutes. Cool slightly and blend until smooth. Return to the pan with the stock, salt, pepper and nutmeg. Bring to the boil, cover and simmer for 15 minutes. Just before serving, stir in the cream. Chop the cheese in a blender and sprinkle generously over each portion of soup.

Make as above, but chop the onions with the metal blade. Grate the cheese with the grating attachment.

French Onion Soup

450g/1lb onions
50g/2oz butter
15ml/1 tablespoon cooking oil
900ml/1½ pints stock
salt and pepper
1 large sprig of parsley
50g/2oz Cheddar cheese
4 thick slices French bread

Skin and quarter the onions and slice them (slicing disc). Melt the butter and oil together in a pan and stir in the sliced onions. Cook over low heat until soft and golden but not browned. Add stock, salt and pepper and simmer for 20 minutes. Chop the parsley (metal blade). Grate the cheese (grating disc). Toast the bread slices on one side. Sprinkle cheese on the other side and toast until bubbling. Pour the soup into serving bowls and float a toast slice in each.

Make as above, but slice the onions with the slicing attachment of a mixer. If not available, chop the onions in a blender. Grate the cheese with the grating attachment of a mixer, or chop finely in a blender.

Right Vichyssoise (pages 28-9)

Gazpacho

900g/2lb ripe tomatoes
2 large Spanish onions
2 garlic cloves
60ml/4 tablespoons olive oil
salt and pepper
a pinch of celery salt
150ml/¼ pint dry sherry
15ml/1 tablespoon tarragon
    vinegar
1 cucumber
450g/1lb green, red and
    yellow peppers
4 large ripe tomatoes
1 small loaf white bread

Cut the tomatoes in half and put into a large pan. Skin the onions and slice them (slicing disc). Skin and crush the garlic. Add the onions and garlic to the tomatoes. Cover with water, add the oil, salt and pepper, celery salt, sherry and vinegar and bring to the boil. Cover and simmer for 1 hour. Cool and blend. Put through a sieve to remove pips and skin, and pour into a serving bowl. Chill for at least 2 hours before serving.

To make the garnishes, peel the cucumber and chop coarsely (metal blade). Remove stems, seeds and membranes from the peppers and chop the flesh coarsely (metal blade), mixing the different colours. Skin the tomatoes by dipping them in boiling water; cut them in quarters and discard the pips; chop the flesh coarsely (metal blade). Remove the crusts from the bread; cut the bread into 1cm/½in dice and put on a baking sheet; bake at 150°C/300°F/Gas Mark 2 for 5 minutes. Put the cucumber, peppers, tomatoes and bread into individual serving dishes. Serve the chilled soup with the side dishes for garnishing.

Make as above, but slice the onions with the slicing attachment of a mixer, or chop in a blender. Chop all the other vegetables in a blender.

Leek and Potato Soup

450g/1lb young leeks
450g/1lb potatoes
50g/2oz butter
750ml/1¼ pints chicken stock
6 stems chives
300ml/½ pint milk
salt and pepper

Wash the leeks thoroughly, remove green tops and slice the white parts (slicing disc). Keep on one side. Peel the potatoes and slice them (slicing disc). Melt the butter in a pan and stir the leeks over low heat for 5 minutes. Add the potatoes and continue cooking for 3 minutes, stirring well. Add the stock and bring to the boil. Cover and simmer for 20 minutes. Chop the chives (metal blade).

The soup may be served in two ways. *Either* stir in the milk, season to taste, re-heat and serve with a garnish of chopped chives *or* blend until smooth and then re-heat with milk and seasoning before serving with chopped chives.

Make as above, but slice the leeks and potatoes with the slicing attachment of a mixer, or chop in a blender.

Vichyssoise
Follow the instructions for Leek and Potato Soup until the soup has simmered for 20 minutes, then blend until smooth. Add milk and seasoning and re-heat. Pour into a bowl, cover and chill until serving time. Stir in 150ml/$\frac{1}{4}$ pint single cream and serve garnished with chopped chives.

Lentil Soup with Frankfurters

350g/12oz lentils (or split peas)
6 ripe tomatoes
1 carrot
1 onion
1·8 litres/3 pints bacon stock
salt and pepper
2 frankfurter sausages

Soak the lentils or split peas for 12 hours in cold water. Skin the tomatoes by dipping them in boiling water. Cut them in quarters and discard the pips. Chop the flesh coarsely (metal blade). Peel the carrot and onion and chop them coarsely (metal blade). Drain the lentils or split peas and put them in a saucepan. Add the tomatoes, carrot and onion. Pour in the bacon stock, and add salt and pepper if required. (If the stock is very salty, do not add extra salt.) Bring to the boil, cover and simmer for 1 hour until the lentils are soft. Cool slightly and blend until smooth. Slice the frankfurters in thick pieces and add to the soup. Re-heat, and season to taste.

Make as above, but chop the tomatoes, carrot and onion in a blender.

Minestrone

Minestrone

75g/3oz dried haricot beans
1·8 litres/3 pints beef or
   bacon stock
100g/4oz smoked bacon
1 large carrot
1 onion
¼ small cabbage
225g/8oz potatoes
1 garlic clove
225g/8oz canned tomatoes
100g/4oz frozen peas
a pinch of dried rosemary
salt and pepper
75g/3oz pasta
3 sprigs parsley
25g/1oz Parmesan or Cheddar
   cheese

Put the beans into a bowl, cover with cold water and leave to soak overnight. Drain the beans and put them into a pan with the stock. Bring to the boil, cover and simmer for 1 hour. Chop the bacon (metal blade) and heat the pieces in a small pan until the fat runs and the bacon is golden-brown. Drain off the excess fat, and put the bacon into the stock. Slice the carrot, onion and cabbage (slicing disc). Chop the potatoes coarsely (metal blade). Crush the garlic. Add all these vegetables and the garlic to the stock. Add the tomatoes and their juice. Cover and simmer for 35 minutes. Stir in the peas, rosemary, salt and pepper, and simmer for 5 minutes. Add pasta shapes or small pieces of macaroni, spaghetti or vermicelli. Cook for 10-12 minutes until the pasta is tender. Chop the parsley (metal blade) and grate the cheese (grating disc). Serve the soup in a tureen or individual bowls and sprinkle with the parsley and cheese.

Make as above, but chop the bacon in a blender. Slice the carrot, onion and cabbage with the slicing attachment of a mixer, or chop in a blender. Chop the potatoes in a blender.

Split Pea Soup

100g/4oz split peas
1 large onion
1 medium carrot
1 medium turnip
1 bacon rasher, without rind
25g/1oz butter
5ml/1 teaspoon sugar
900ml/1½ pints stock
300ml/½ pint milk
salt and pepper

Put the split peas into a blender, cover and blend for 1 minute. Skin the onion, carrot and turnip. Cut the vegetables and bacon into small pieces. Melt the butter and cook the onion and bacon until golden-brown. Add the carrot and turnip and cook for 2 minutes, stirring well. Add the peas, sugar and stock, and simmer for 45 minutes. Pour into the blender, add the milk and blend for 1 minute. Return to the saucepan and re-heat, seasoning with salt and pepper to taste. Garnish with small cubes of fried bread.

Make as above, but process the split peas until finely chopped, with the metal blade. Chop the vegetables and bacon with the metal blade. Process the cooked vegetables and peas with a little cooking liquid until smooth, using the metal blade, then add to the remaining liquid and milk.

Watercress Soup

1 bunch watercress
450g/1lb potatoes
900ml/1½ pints chicken stock
300ml/½ pint milk
15g/½oz cornflour
salt and pepper

Wash the watercress and keep a few leaves for garnish. Cut the potatoes into pieces and cook in the chicken stock for 25 minutes. Put into a blender with the watercress, cover and blend until smooth. Add the milk and the cornflour mixed with a little milk or water, and blend for 10 seconds. Re-heat the soup, seasoning to taste, and garnish with the reserved watercress leaves.

Make as above, but chop the potatoes coarsely using the metal blade. Process the cooked potatoes, watercress and a little cooking liquid until smooth, using the metal blade, then adding the remaining liquid and milk.

Pâtés

Pâtés and terrines made from meat, poultry, game or fish may be used as first courses, or can be a complete light meal when served with salad or toast.

The container for the pâté should be placed in an oven roasting tin containing hot water to come half-way up the dish, as this will mean that the pâté is cooked in a low moist heat and will not dry out. It is cooked when it has shrunk slightly from the sides of the container and when a knitting needle or sharp knife comes out clean. Juices which run out should be clear, not pink, but the meat should still retain a slightly pink tinge, rather than one which is grey. When the pâté is cooked, cover with stout card, then foil and place weights on top, or tins of food. Leave for at least 6 hours in a cold place so that the pâté will be firm enough to cut neatly. It will, in fact, be at its best if left for 24 hours since the flavours will have blended and matured.

Chicken Liver Pâté

225g/8oz chicken livers
1 small onion
75g/3oz fat bacon
25g/1oz butter
2 garlic cloves
1 egg
salt and pepper
50g/2oz clarified butter

Cut the livers into pieces and chop finely (metal blade). Keep on one side. Skin the onion. Cut the bacon and onion into pieces and chop finely (metal blade). Melt the butter and cook the onion and bacon gently for 5 minutes. Skin the garlic cloves. Put the livers, onion, bacon, butter juices, garlic, egg, salt and pepper into the bowl and process until smooth (plastic blade). Put into an ovenproof container, and cover with a lid or foil. Cook at 180°C/350°F/Gas Mark 4 for 1 hour. Remove the lid. Cover and weight the pâté. Leave for 4 hours until cold. Melt the clarified butter and pour it over the surface to cover the pâté completely. Leave until the butter has set firmly. Serve with toast.

Make as above, but cook the roughly chopped onion and butter before chopping finely in a blender. Add the remaining ingredients in small quantities until smoothly blended.

Game Terrine

675g/1½lb mixed uncooked
  game
100g/4oz fat bacon
45ml/3 tablespoons brandy
350g/12oz lean pork
salt and pepper
a pinch of ground nutmeg
a pinch of dried mixed herbs
1 egg

Remove skin from the game and cut the flesh in small pieces. Cut the bacon into pieces. Cut them both coarsely in the bowl (metal blade) and tip into a basin with the brandy. Leave to stand for 1 hour. Cut the pork into small pieces and then chop very finely (metal blade). Mix with the game, bacon and brandy. Season well with salt, pepper, nutmeg and herbs and stir in the egg until well blended. Put into an ovenproof container and cover with a lid or foil. Cook at 180°C/350°F/Gas Mark 4 for 1½ hours. Remove the lid. Cover and weight the pâté. Leave for 24 hours before serving in slices with salad or toast.

Note Try to have a mixture of light and dark meat, and if little light meat is available, add a chicken joint to the game. Pheasant, pigeon, hare and rabbit are all good in a mixed game pâté.

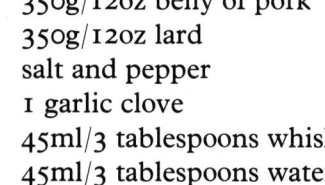

Make as above, but mince the game, bacon and pork through the coarse screen of a mincing attachment.

Hazelnut Pâté

450g/1lb pig's liver
350g/12oz belly of pork
350g/12oz lard
salt and pepper
1 garlic clove
45ml/3 tablespoons whisky
45ml/3 tablespoons water
100g/4oz unsalted shelled
  hazelnuts

Cut the liver and pork into pieces and chop finely (metal blade). Mix with slightly softened lard, salt and pepper, crushed garlic, whisky, the water and hazelnuts. Leave to stand for 1 hour. Put into an ovenproof container and cover with greaseproof paper and foil. Cook at 160°C/325°F/Gas Mark 3 for 2 hours. Cover and weight lightly until completely cold. This pâté is best eaten after two or three days, and may be served in slices with salad or with toast.

Make as above, but mince the liver and pork through the fine screen of a mincing attachment.

Kipper Pâté

225g/8oz kipper fillets
25g/1oz melted butter
juice of $\frac{1}{2}$ lemon
1 garlic clove
15ml/1 tablespoon brandy
4 drops Tabasco sauce
30ml/2 tablespoons single
    cream

Cook the kippers by grilling or poaching them. Remove the skin and larger bones. Break the flesh into the blender with the melted butter, lemon juice, garlic clove, brandy and Tabasco sauce. Blend until smooth. Add the cream and blend for 2 seconds. Put into a serving dish and chill before serving.

Make as above, but process until smooth, using the metal or plastic blade.

Lamb Pâté

350g/12oz streaky bacon
    rashers, without rinds
350g/12oz lamb's liver
800g/1¾lb shoulder lamb
1 large onion
1 garlic clove
1 tablespoon concentrated
    tomato purée
5ml/1 teaspoon sage
5ml/1 teaspoon rosemary
salt and pepper
100g/4oz melted butter
150ml/¼ pint red wine

Stretch the bacon rashers with a palette knife. Line a casserole or terrine with them. Mince together the liver, lamb, onion and garlic. Mix with the remaining ingredients and put into the bacon-lined dish. Fold the bacon over the top and cover with foil. Cook at 180°C/350°F/Gas Mark 4 for 1½ hours. Cool and weight for 24 hours. If liked, decorate with thin orange slices and a thin glaze of aspic jelly.

Make as above, but chop the liver, lamb, onion and garlic finely, using the metal blade.

Pork and Spinach Pâté

1 bay leaf
225g/8oz streaky bacon
    rashers, without rinds
225g/8oz belly of pork
100g/4oz back bacon
1 small onion
½ garlic clove
1 sprig of parsley
2·5ml/½ teaspoon fresh
    rosemary
1 size 6 egg
225g/8oz spinach
pepper

Grease a loaf tin or terrine and put the bay leaf in it. Stretch the bacon rashers with a palette knife. Use two-thirds to line the terrine. Cut the pork and back bacon into small pieces and chop finely (metal blade). Skin the onion and garlic, cut into pieces and add them to the meat. Process until finely chopped. Take out half the mixture and keep on one side. Add the parsley, rosemary and egg to the bowl and process until the mixture is creamy. Keep on one side. Wash the spinach and put into a saucepan. Cover and cook over high heat (do not add any water) for 4-5 minutes until just tender. Drain off surplus liquid. Put into the mixer bowl and chop finely but do not mix to a purée (metal blade). Mix the spinach with the two meat mixtures and season well with

(CONTINUES)

pepper. Put into the lined dish, cover with the remaining bacon rashers, then cover with a piece of foil, and a lid. Cook at 160°C/325°F/Gas Mark 3 for 1½ hours. Remove from the roasting tin. Cool and weight the pork. Leave for 24 hours before turning out of the dish. Serve in thick slices with salad.

Make as above, but mince the pork and back bacon with the onion through the fine screen of a mincing attachment. Blend half this mixture with the herbs and egg until smooth. Chop the spinach finely in a blender.

Potted Beef

1 small onion
450g/1lb chuck steak
a pinch of ground mace
a pinch of ground allspice
salt and pepper
1 sprig of parsley
1 sprig of thyme
1 bay leaf
150ml/¼ pint beef stock
50g/2oz butter
15ml/1 tablespoon port or
  sherry
1·25ml/¼ teaspoon anchovy
  essence

Skin the onion and cut it into eighths. Chop finely (metal blade). Put into a casserole. Cut the steak into cubes and add to the casserole with the mace, allspice, salt, pepper, parsley, thyme, bay leaf and stock. Cover and cook at 150°C/300°F/ Gas Mark 2 for 2½ hours. Leave the meat to cool in the stock. Drain the meat, reserving the stock. Discard the herbs. Put the meat into the bowl with 2 tablespoons stock, butter, port or sherry and anchovy essence. Mix until completely smooth (metal blade). Spoon into a serving dish and chill for an hour before serving with toast, or as a sandwich filling.

Make as above, but chop the onion in a blender. Blend the cooked meat with 4 tablespoons stock, the butter, port or sherry and anchovy essence until smooth.

Rich Liver Pâté

350g/12oz pig's liver
5 anchovies
1 small onion
50g/2oz breadcrumbs
450ml/¾ pint milk
225g/8oz lard
50g/2oz butter
50g/2oz plain flour
1 size 1-2 egg
15g/½oz salt

Cut the liver into pieces. Drain the anchovies, and cut the onion into pieces. Mince the liver, anchovies and onion, using the fine screen of the mincer attachment. Soak the crumbs in a little of the milk. Put the liver mixture through the mincer again with the soaked crumbs and the lard. Melt the butter, work in the flour, and cook gently for 3 minutes, stirring well. Add the rest of the milk and cook gently, stirring all the time to make a thick sauce. Cool and then put into the blender with the meat mixture, egg and seasonings.

(CONTINUES)

15g/½oz pepper
5ml/1 teaspoon mixed spice
5ml/1 teaspoon ground cloves
2·5ml/½ teaspoon sugar

Blend until smooth. Put into an ovenproof dish and cover with a piece of foil and a lid. Cook at 180°C/350°F/Gas Mark 4 for 2 hours. Cover and weight for 24 hours.

Make as above, but chop the liver, anchovies and onion finely, using the metal blade. Add the soaked crumbs and lard, and process until well mixed. Add the sauce, egg and seasonings through the feeder tube with the machine running until the mixture is well blended and smooth.

Sardine Pâté

90g/3½oz canned sardines in oil
150g/5oz full fat soft cheese
15ml/1 tablespoon lemon juice
salt and pepper
a pinch of Cayenne pepper
2 hard-boiled eggs

Mix the sardines and oil until broken up (plastic blade). Add the cheese cut into pieces, with the lemon juice, salt, pepper and Cayenne pepper. Continue mixing until well blended. Cut the eggs in pieces and put into the bowl. Mix long enough for the eggs to be finely chopped. Put into a serving dish and chill for an hour before serving. Serve with toast or in sandwiches.

Make as above, but blend the ingredients in the given order in a blender. Add the eggs and blend only until the eggs are finely chopped.

Seafood Pâté

450g/1lb fresh prawns or shrimps
450g/1lb haddock
50g/2oz softened butter
5ml/1 teaspoon anchovy essence
a pinch of ground mace
a pinch of Cayenne pepper
100g/4oz clarified butter

Shell the prawns or shrimps and put the shells into a saucepan. Add just enough liquid to cover and bring to the boil. Strain the liquid and put into a saucepan. Discard the shells. Cut the haddock in pieces and add to the liquid. Simmer for 10 minutes until tender. Chop the prawns or shrimps coarsely in a blender and put into a bowl. Drain the haddock and break into large flakes. Put into the blender with the butter, anchovy essence, mace and Cayenne pepper. Blend until smooth. Add to the prawns or shrimps and stir in until well mixed (the creamy fish mixture should be stuffed with large pieces of pink shellfish). Put into a serving dish. Chill for 1 hour. Melt the clarified butter and pour it over the chilled mixture. Chill for an hour before serving with toast.

(CONTINUES)

Make as on page 37, but chop the prawns or shrimps coarsely using the metal blade. Mix the haddock with the butter, essence and seasonings until smooth, using the plastic blade, then mix with the chopped prawns or shrimps.

Smoked Fish Pâté

2 smoked trout or mackerel
150ml/¼ pint soured cream
100g/4oz cottage cheese
juice of ½ lemon
salt and pepper

Skin the fish and remove the flesh. Put into the blender with the other ingredients and blend until smooth. Put into small individual dishes and chill. Serve with thin slices of toast made from brown bread, and slices of lemon.

Make as above, processing the ingredients until smooth with the metal or plastic blade.

Below Smoked Fish Pâté
Right Pork and Spinach Pâté (pages 35-36)

Smoked Salmon Pâté

450g/1lb smoked salmon
50g/2oz unsalted butter
15ml/1 tablespoon lemon
   juice
15ml/1 tablespoon dry sherry
a pinch of pepper
150ml/¼ pint double cream

Chop the salmon finely (metal blade). Soften the butter slightly, but do not let it melt. Add to the salmon with the lemon juice, sherry and pepper. Mix until just smooth (plastic blade). Add the cream and mix again until light and creamy. Put into a serving dish and chill for an hour before serving with toast or on canapés.

Note Smoked salmon trimmings may sometimes be bought for preparing this pâté.

Make as above, but put all the ingredients except the cream into a blender and blend until smooth. Add the cream, and blend until light and creamy.

Taramasalata

225g/8oz smoked cod's roe
2 thin slices white bread
   (large loaf)
30ml/2 tablespoons milk
2 garlic cloves
150ml/¼ pint olive oil
30ml/2 tablespoons lemon
   juice
pepper
30ml/2 tablespoons double
   cream or natural yoghurt

The cod's roe may be fresh or from a jar. If fresh, remove the skin before processing. Discard the crusts and soak the bread in the milk for 10 minutes. Blend until smooth. Skin the garlic and blend with the cod's roe and soaked bread. With the machine running, pour in the oil slowly until the mixture looks like mayonnaise. Add the lemon juice, pepper, cream or yoghurt and blend until just mixed. Place in a serving dish and chill for an hour before serving with toast.

Make as above, but mix the garlic with the cod's roe and soaked bread until very smooth, using the metal blade. Pour in the oil through the feeder tube, using the metal blade. Mix the lemon juice, pepper, cream or yoghurt until just combined, using the plastic blade.

Turkey Terrine

350g/12oz cooked turkey
30ml/2 tablespoons brandy
225g/8oz fat pork
60ml/4 tablespoons milk
1 onion
25g/1oz butter
100g/4oz white bread
1 egg
salt and pepper
a pinch of ground nutmeg
a pinch of dried mixed herbs

Cut the turkey into small pieces and chop coarsely in a blender. Put into a bowl with the brandy and leave to stand while processing the other ingredients. Cut the pork into small pieces and blend with the milk. Keep on one side. Skin the onion, cut into quarters and chop finely in a blender. Melt the butter and cook the onion until soft and golden. Mix the onion and butter with the pork. Blend the bread with the pork, onion, butter, egg, salt, pepper, nutmeg and herbs. Put half the mixture in a greased ovenproof container and top with turkey pieces, sprinkling with brandy. Cover with the remaining mixture, then cover with a lid or piece of foil. Cook at 180°C/350°F/Gas Mark 4 for 1¼ hours. Remove the lid, cover and weight the pâté. Leave for 24 hours before serving in slices with a salad.

Note This is an excellent way of using up leftover Christmas turkey, but the terrine can, of course, be made with an individual turkey joint or rolled turkey which is now available. Use a mixture of dark and light meat from the turkey.

Make as above, but chop the cooked turkey coarsely, using the metal blade. Chop the pork finely with the metal blade. Chop the onion finely with the metal blade. Soak the bread in the milk for 10 minutes and thoroughly mix with the pork, onion, butter, egg, seasoning, nutmeg and herbs, using the plastic blade.

Main Courses, Vegetables and Salads

Apricot Pork with Apple Sauce

100g/4oz white bread
a sprig of parsley
1 × 425g/15oz can apricot
   halves
2·5ml/½ teaspoon fresh mixed
   herbs
1 egg
salt and pepper
1·8kg/4lb boned pork joint
350g/12oz cooking apples
25g/1oz Demerara sugar

Make breadcrumbs in the blender, adding the parsley with the last batch of bread. Put into a mixing bowl. Drain the apricots and blend half of them until they are roughly chopped. Mix with the bread, herbs, egg and seasonings, and stir well. Stuff the meat and put it into a roasting tin. Pour over the apricot syrup and cook at 190°C/375°F/Gas Mark 5 for 2½ hours, basting with syrup once or twice. Peel and core the apples and chop them roughly in the blender. Put into a saucepan with 90ml/6 tablespoons water and Demerara sugar and cook until soft. Put into the blender and add the remaining apricots. Blend until smooth and re-heat just before serving with the pork.

Make as above, preparing the breadcrumbs with the metal blade, and adding the parsley with the last batch of bread. Remove to a bowl and then chop half the apricots with the metal blade. When making the sauce, chop the apples roughly with the metal blade. Process the cooked apples and remaining apricots with the plastic blade.

Baked Cheese Pudding

175g/6oz day-old white bread
100g/4oz Cheddar cheese
1 small onion
600ml/1 pint milk
50g/2oz butter
2 eggs, separated
salt and pepper

Discard the crusts from the bread and make bread into crumbs (metal blade). Grate the cheese (grating disc). Chop the onion finely (metal blade). Put the milk and butter into a pan and heat until the butter has just melted. Pour over the bread and leave to soak for 30 minutes. Stir in the egg yolks, cheese and onion, and season well. Whisk the egg whites to stiff peaks and fold into the crumbs. Grease an ovenproof dish and fill with the cheese mixture. Bake at 180°C/350°F/

(CONTINUES)

Gas Mark 4 for 1 hour. Serve hot with vegetables, or leave until cold, turn out and serve with salad.

Make as above, preparing the breadcrumbs in a blender. Chop the cheese finely in a blender or in the grating attachment of a mixer; chop the onion in a blender. Whisk the egg whites with a mixer.

Baked Gammon in Apple Sauce

450g/1lb gammon steak,
   5cm/2in thick
25g/1oz butter
3 medium onions
150ml/¼ pint dry cider
2 medium cooking apples
50g/2oz soft brown sugar
5ml/1 teaspoon mustard
   powder
pepper
3 cloves

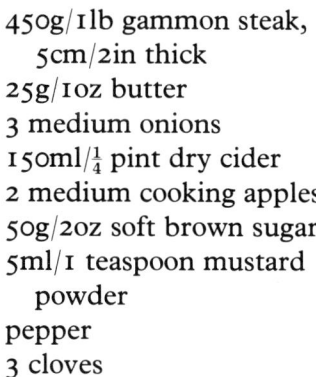

Put the gammon steak into an ovenproof dish well-greased with the butter. Cut the onions in pieces and put into the blender with the cider, peeled and cored apples, sugar, mustard and pepper. Blend until the onions and apples are finely chopped. Pour the mixture over the gammon and add the cloves. Cover with foil and bake at 180°C/350°F/Gas Mark 4 for 1 hour. Uncover the gammon, remove the cloves and continue baking for 15 minutes.

Make as above, using the metal blade to chop the onions with the cider, apples, sugar, mustard and pepper.

Baked Stuffed Mackerel

4 mackerel
1 onion
25g/1oz butter
1 apple
75g/3oz fresh white bread
2·5ml/½ teaspoon mixed herbs
grated rind and juice of ½
   lemon
salt and pepper

Open each fish and press out the backbone. Skin the onion and chop it finely in the blender. Cook in the butter until soft but not coloured. Peel the apple and chop it in the blender. Make breadcrumbs in the blender. Mix together the onion, apple, breadcrumbs, herbs, lemon rind and juice, salt and pepper. Divide the stuffing between the fish, and roll up from the wide end, securing with a cocktail stick. Put in an ovenproof dish and brush each fish with a little oil. Cover with a piece of foil or a lid and bake at 180°C/350°F/Gas Mark 4 for 30 minutes. Remove the foil or lid and continue cooking for 5 minutes. Serve garnished with lemon slices and sprigs of parsley, and with thin brown bread and butter.

Make as above, chopping the onion finely with the metal blade. Chop the apples with the metal blade. Prepare the breadcrumbs with the metal blade.

Bakehouse Lamb

675g/1½lb potatoes
225g/8oz onions
salt and pepper
1·8kg/4lb leg of lamb
60ml/4 tablespoons mint jelly
100g/4oz day-old white bread
2 large sprigs parsley

Peel the potatoes and slice them with the slicing attachment of a mixer. Skin the onions and chop them coarsely in a blender. Arrange half the potatoes in a layer on the base of a greased ovenproof dish. Season with salt and pepper. Sprinkle with the onions and then put on the remaining potatoes. Place the leg of lamb on top of this bed of vegetables. Do not add any fat as there will be enough in the lamb for roasting the meat and vegetables. Sprinkle the skin of the lamb with salt and pepper. Roast at 190°C/375°F/Gas Mark 5 for 1 hour. Baste the vegetables with the fat from the lamb. Spread the mint jelly on the lamb skin. Discard the crusts and prepare breadcrumbs in a blender with the parsley. Season with salt and pepper and press all over the skin of the lamb. Sprinkle a little fat on the crumbs. Continue roasting for 45 minutes. Remove the lamb to a carving dish and serve the vegetables from the ovenproof dish.

Make as above, preparing the potatoes with the slicing disc. Chop the onions coarsely with the metal blade. Prepare the breadcrumbs with the metal blade.

Beef Croquettes

350g/12oz cooked beef
100g/4oz day-old white bread
25g/1oz pickled cucumber
25g/1oz plain flour
150ml/¼ pint milk
25g/1oz butter
10ml/2 teaspoons chopped
　　fresh herbs
salt and pepper
50g/2oz hard bread
1 egg
oil for deep frying

Cut the beef into pieces and chop finely (metal blade). Discard the crusts and make the bread into crumbs (metal blade). Chop the cucumber (metal blade). Blend the flour and milk together (plastic blade). Melt the butter in a pan and stir in the milk mixture. Cook over low heat, stirring well, until thick and creamy. Mix in the meat, bread, cucumber, herbs, salt and pepper. Leave until cold and then form into 8 sausage shapes. Break the hard bread into pieces and make into breadcrumbs (metal blade). Beat the egg lightly with a fork and coat each croquette with egg, then coat with breadcrumbs. Fry in hot oil until crisp and brown. Serve hot with vegetables or cold with salad.

Make as above, but chop the beef with a little of the milk in a blender. The cucumber may also be added to the beef for chopping as the liquid in it will make it easier to chop the beef. Blend the flour and milk in a blender. Prepare breadcrumbs in a blender.

Beef Fritters

100g/4oz plain flour
1·25ml/¼ teaspoon salt
1 egg
90ml/6 tablespoons beer
450g/1lb raw minced beef
1 medium onion
2·5ml/½ teaspoon mixed herbs
15ml/1 tablespoon
    concentrated tomato purée
15ml/1 tablespoon French
    mustard
salt and pepper

Make a batter by putting the flour, salt, egg and beer into the blender and blending until thick and creamy (it is best to put the flour into the blender last). Mix together the beef, grated onion, herbs, tomato purée, mustard, salt and pepper very thoroughly and divide into 8 pieces. Shape into balls and press out into thin rounds on a floured surface. Dip into the batter and fry in hot fat or oil for 15 minutes, turning once. Drain well on absorbent paper and serve with tomato sauce.

Note The batter can be made with milk, but beer gives a light crisp fritter.

Make as above, but chop the onion finely with the metal blade. Make the batter using the plastic blade.

Cabbage and Carrot Coleslaw

450g/1lb firm white cabbage
2 celery sticks
½ small onion
2 carrots
1 eating apple
50g/2oz walnut halves
60ml/4 tablespoons
    mayonnaise
30ml/2 tablespoons single
    cream
15ml/1 tablespoon vinegar
a pinch of mustard powder

Wash and trim the cabbage and celery. Skin the onion, carrots and apple, and remove the apple core. Shred the cabbage, slice the onion and celery (slicing disc). Grate the carrots (grating disc). Grate the apple (grating disc). Put all the prepared vegetables into a bowl. Chop the walnuts (metal blade). Add the apple and nuts to the vegetables. Stir together the mayonnaise, cream, vinegar and mustard. Pour over the other ingredients and toss well so that the dressing is mixed right through the salad.

Make as above, using the shredding and grating attachments of a mixer. Chop the walnuts in a blender.

Cheese and Onion Casserole

6 slices white bread
175g/6oz Cheddar cheese
3 eggs
salt and pepper
1 small onion
400ml/¾ pint lukewarm milk

Remove the crusts from the bread and cut the bread into triangles. Put half the triangles into a greased ovenproof dish. Grate the cheese and sprinkle two-thirds of it over the bread. Cover with the remaining bread triangles. Put the eggs, seasoning, chopped onion and milk into the blender, and blend until the onion is finely chopped. Pour over the bread and leave to stand for 30 minutes. Sprinkle with the remaining cheese, bake at 180°C/350°F/Gas Mark 4 for 1 hour until well browned, and serve very hot.

Make as above, but chop the cheese finely with the metal blade. Mix the eggs, seasoning, onion and milk with the metal blade until the onion is finely chopped.

Cheshire Pork Pie

225g/8oz plain flour
a pinch of salt
50g/2oz block margarine
50g/2oz lard
45-60ml/3-4 tablespoons cold
  water
900g/2lb lean pork
4 eating apples
salt and pepper
a pinch of ground nutmeg
25g/1oz sugar
150ml/¼ pint dry white wine
  or dry cider
75g/3oz butter
beaten egg for glazing

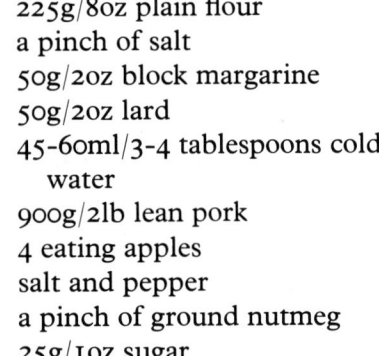

Put the flour and salt into the mixer bowl (plastic blade). Cut the fats into cubes and add to the flour. Mix for 10 seconds until the mixture is like fine breadcrumbs. With the machine switched on, add just enough water through the feeder tube to make a firm dough. Roll the pastry into 2 circles to fit a 25cm/10in pie plate.

Cut the meat into pieces and chop (metal blade). Peel and core the apples and slice (slicing disc). Line the plate with one piece of pastry. Put in half the pork and season with salt, pepper and nutmeg. Put the apples on top and sprinkle with sugar. Top with the remaining pork and season with salt, pepper and nutmeg. Pour over the wine or cider and dot the pork with flakes of butter. Cover with the remaining pastry and cut a slit on top. Surround with pastry leaves made from trimmings. Add a pinch of salt to the beaten egg and use to brush the pastry. Bake at 220°C/425°F/Gas Mark 7 for 15 minutes. Reduce the heat to 190°C/375°F/Gas Mark 5 for a further 45 minutes. Serve hot.

Make as above, but prepare the pastry with a mixer. Slice the apples with the slicing attachment, or chop coarsely in a blender.

Cabbage and Carrot Coleslaw (page 45)

Chicken Cannelloni

8 pieces cannelloni
1 onion
1 garlic clove
100g/4oz button mushrooms
30ml/2 tablespoons oil
225g/8oz cooked chicken
15g/½oz day-old white bread
25g/1oz Parmesan cheese
5ml/1 teaspoon chopped fresh
   marjoram
1 egg
salt and pepper

Sauce
50g/2oz butter
40g/1½oz plain flour
300ml/½ pint milk
150ml/¼ pint single cream
salt and white pepper
a pinch of grated nutmeg
25g/1oz Parmesan cheese

Bring a large pan of salted water to the boil and put in the cannelloni. Stir for a minute so that it does not stick together. Cook for about 10 minutes until just tender. Drain well and leave to cool while preparing the filling.

Skin the onion and garlic and chop finely (metal blade). Wipe the mushrooms and chop coarsely (metal blade). Heat the oil in a pan and cook the onion, garlic and mushrooms for 5 minutes over low heat, stirring well. Cut the chicken into pieces and chop very finely (metal blade). Discard the crusts, cut the bread into pieces and make into crumbs (metal blade), grate the cheese (grating disc). Stir the chicken into the onion mixture with the breadcrumbs, cheese and marjoram. Remove from the heat and work in the egg, salt and pepper. Cool and then divide the filling between the pieces of pasta. Roll up lengthways. Arrange the pasta in a buttered ovenproof dish.

To make the sauce, mix 40g/1½oz butter, the flour and the milk until smooth (plastic blade). Pour into a pan, bring to the boil and simmer for 3 minutes, stirring all the time. Stir in the cream and heat gently, stirring well. Season with salt, pepper and nutmeg. Spoon over the pasta and dot with flakes of the remaining butter. Grate the cheese (grating disc) and sprinkle it over the pasta. Bake at 190°C/375°F/Gas Mark 5 for 30 minutes. Serve as a first course, or as a main course with green salad and crusty bread.

Make as above, but chop the onion, garlic and mushrooms in a blender. Chop the chicken finely in a blender. Prepare the breadcrumbs in a blender. Grate the cheese with the slicing attachment of a mixer, or chop finely in a blender.

For the sauce, blend together the butter, flour and milk in a blender. Chop the cheese in a blender.

Chicken Vol-au-vents

12 × 7.5cm/3in vol-au-vent
   cases
25g/1oz butter
25g/1oz plain flour
150ml/¼ pint chicken stock

Bake the vol-au-vent cases. Melt the butter. Put the flour, chicken stock and milk in the blender and blend until smooth. Pour on to the butter and stir over gentle heat until the mixture boils. Simmer for 2 minutes, stirring well. Return to the blender with the chicken cut in pieces, green pepper, cream,

(CONTINUES)

150ml/¼ pint milk
225g/8oz cooked chicken
1 small green pepper
30ml/2 tablespoons single
    cream
2·5ml/½ teaspoon Tabasco
    sauce
salt and pepper

Tabasco sauce, salt and pepper, and blend until the chicken is finely chopped. Return to the saucepan and simmer for 8 minutes. Fill the vol-au-vent cases with the mixture and serve hot. If liked, a few mushrooms may be added to the mixture, or ham or seafood may be substituted for the chicken.

Make as above, but use the plastic blade to mix the sauce. Change to the metal blade to process the chicken, pepper, cream and seasonings until the chicken is finely chopped.

Country Pork

1·8kg/4lb loin of pork
1 onion
1 eating apple
6 sage leaves
75g/3oz day-old white bread
1 egg
15ml/1 tablespoon lemon
    juice
salt and pepper
a little oil

Have the joint boned, and ask the butcher to score the skin finely. Make a slit in the meat where the bone has been removed so that the stuffing can be inserted. Skin the onion, and peel and core the apple. Mix them with the sage leaves and chop finely (metal blade). Discard the crusts and make the bread into crumbs (metal blade). Add to the onion mixture and add the egg, lemon juice, salt and pepper. Mix well and insert into the meat. Tie the joint in 3 or 4 places with string. Put into a roasting tin and rub a little oil over the skin. Sprinkle with salt and rub in. Roast at 180°C/350°F/Gas Mark 4 for 2½ hours.

Make as above, chopping the onion, apple and sage in a blender. Prepare the breadcrumbs in a blender.

Fish Cakes

450g/1lb cooked fish
2 size 1-2 eggs
25g/1oz plain flour
30ml/2 tablespoons lemon
    juice
30ml/2 tablespoons parsley
5ml/1 teaspoon
    Worcestershire sauce
40g/1½oz melted butter
salt and pepper
450g/1lb mashed potatoes
beaten egg
breadcrumbs

Break the fish into small pieces and put into the blender with the eggs, flour, lemon juice, parsley, Worcestershire sauce, butter and seasoning. Cover and blend until the fish is well broken up. Work the mixture into the mashed potatoes. Divide into 16 pieces and make into round flat cakes. Coat with beaten egg and breadcrumbs, and fry until golden.

Make as above, but prepare the fish mixture, using the plastic blade.

Glazed Carrots

450g/1lb carrots
300ml/½ pint chicken stock
25g/1oz butter
10ml/2 teaspoons sugar
a pinch of salt
1 sprig of parsley

Scrape the carrots and slice them with the slicing attachment of a mixer. Put into a pan with the other ingredients except the parsley. Bring to the boil, cover and cook for 5 minutes. Remove the lid and simmer until tender and the stock is absorbed. Chop the parsley and sprinkle over the carrots.

Make as above, preparing the carrots with the slicing disc.

Golden Salad

4 medium carrots
50g/2oz salted peanuts
mayonnaise
green salad
4 pineapple rings

Shred the carrots and peanuts coarsely using the shredding attachment of the mixer, and mix with enough mayonnaise to moisten. Put the green salad on to plates, top with pineapple rings and then the carrot and nut mixture.

Make as above, shredding the carrots with the grating disc. Chop the peanuts coarsely with the metal blade.

Home-made Sausages

225g/8oz lean pork
225g/8oz fat belly of pork
1 garlic clove
4 sage leaves
a pinch of dried thyme
2·5ml/½ teaspoon salt
5ml/1 teaspoon pepper

Cut the lean and fat pork into pieces. Skin and chop the garlic. Chop the pork, garlic and sage leaves, coarsely or finely according to taste (metal blade). Add the thyme, salt and pepper, and process just long enough to mix. Form into about 16 sausage shapes or flat patties. Chill in the refrigerator for 12 hours before using so that the flavours blend and mature.

Make as above, using the coarse or fine screen of mincing attachment of a mixer. Use the sausage-filling attachment to fill sausage skins.

Honeyed Almond Roast Chicken

25g/1oz dried apricots
25g/1oz blanched almonds
1 small onion
25g/1oz butter
50g/2oz white bread
2·5ml/$\frac{1}{2}$ teaspoon thyme
15ml/1 tablespoon clear
   honey
1 egg
1·4-1·8kg/3-4lb chicken
15ml/1 tablespoon oil
a pinch of salt
a sprig of rosemary

Soak the apricots in water for 3 hours and drain. Put them in the blender with the almonds and blend on low speed until the almonds are finely chopped. Remove and put into a bowl. Chop the onion in the blender and cook in the butter until soft and golden. Add to the bowl with the apricots. Break the bread into small pieces and put into the blender with the thyme. Blend to make breadcrumbs. Put into the bowl and add the honey. Mix together and add about half the egg to make a light, crumbly stuffing. Put the stuffing in the neck of the bird under the skin flap. Brush the chicken with the oil, sprinkle with salt and put the sprig of rosemary on top. Cover with foil and bake at 200°C/400°F/Gas Mark 6, allowing 20 minutes per ·5kg/1lb and 20 minutes extra. Remove the foil 15 minutes before the end of the cooking time to allow the bird to brown.

Make as above, chopping the apricots and almonds with the metal blade. Chop the onion with the metal blade. Prepare the breadcrumbs with the metal blade.

Jellied Parsley Gammon

900g/2lb middle gammon
1 beef bone
3 pig's trotters
1 onion
2 bay leaves
3 sprigs tarragon
1 sprig of thyme
a large bunch of parsley
1 × 75ml bottle dry white
   wine
1 egg white plus unbroken
   egg shell
15ml/1 tablespoon white
   wine vinegar

Soak the gammon in cold water for 3 hours and drain well. Meanwhile, put the beef bone, trotters, onion, bay leaves, tarragon, thyme and 1 parsley sprig into a pan. Reserve 150ml/$\frac{1}{4}$ pint wine and pour the rest into the pan, adding a little water if necessary to cover the bones. Bring to the boil, cover and then simmer for 3 hours. Add the gammon and continue simmering for 1$\frac{1}{4}$ hours until tender. Lift out the gammon and cut into pieces. Chop lean and fat coarsely (metal blade) and press lightly into a glass bowl. Strain the stock through a fine sieve and leave until cold. Remove all fat from the surface. Heat the stock until it melts completely. Whisk the egg white lightly. Wash the egg shell and crush into small pieces. Add to the stock with the egg white. Bring gently to the boil and boil hard for 2 minutes, whisking to make the stock foamy. Remove from the heat, cover and leave to stand for 15 minutes. Strain through some filter paper or 3 thicknesses of kitchen paper in a sieve. Pour a little of this clear stock over the meat to moisten it. Chill the remaining stock in the refrigerator and when it is just setting,

(CONTINUES)

stir in the reserved wine and wine vinegar. Chop the remaining parsley finely (metal blade) and stir into the stock. Pour over the meat and leave it to set. The finished dish consists of small tender pieces of pink and white meat in a beautiful green jelly.

Make as above, chopping the gammon with a little of the liquid in a blender. Chop the parsley finely in a blender.

Kidney Pudding

3 lambs' kidneys
100g/4oz day-old white
     bread
1 sprig of parsley
15ml/1 tablespoon shredded
     suet
1 egg
75ml/5 tablespoons milk
2·5ml/½ teaspoon dried mixed
     herbs
salt and pepper

Skin the kidneys and remove the cores. Chop finely (metal blade). Discard the crusts, put the bread and parsley in the processor bowl and make into crumbs (metal blade). Mix the bread with the kidneys, suet, egg, milk, herbs, salt and pepper. Put the kidney mixture in a greased pudding basin, cover with greased greaseproof paper and foil and put into a pan. Pour in boiling water to come half-way up the bowl. Cover, and boil for 1½ hours, adding more boiling water if needed so that the pan does not boil dry. Turn out and serve.

Make as above, but chop the kidneys with a little of the milk in a blender. Prepare the breadcrumbs and parsley in a blender.

Lamburgers

1 large onion
25g/1oz butter
450g/1lb shoulder lamb
1 small green pepper
1 celery stick
15ml/1 tablespoon
     concentrated tomato purée
15ml/1 tablespoon tomato
     sauce
5ml/1 teaspoon mixed herbs
2·5ml/½ teaspoon
     Worcestershire sauce
salt and pepper
50g/2oz fresh white
     breadcrumbs

Cut the onion in pieces and blend until finely chopped. Cook gently in the butter until soft and golden but not brown. Mince the lamb and chop the green pepper and celery finely in the blender. Mix all the ingredients together. Turn on to a floured board and divide into 8 pieces. Shape into thick patties. Fry in oil on both sides until golden-brown, which will take about 10-15 minutes. Serve with vegetables or salad. If liked, put each hot lamburger into a warm split soft roll and garnish with tomatoes and watercress.

Make as above, chopping the onion finely with the metal blade. Chop the lamb, green pepper and celery finely together with the metal blade.

Lasagne

450g/1lb raw lean beef
1 small onion
5ml/1 teaspoon dried
    marjoram or sage
15ml/1 tablespoon
    concentrated tomato purée
300ml/½ pint beef stock
salt and pepper
275g/10oz lasagne
75g/3oz Cheddar cheese
25g/1oz butter
25g/1oz plain flour
300ml/½ pint milk
1 egg yolk
a pinch of ground nutmeg
60ml/4 tablespoons single
    cream

Cut the meat into small pieces and skin the onion. Chop them
finely (metal blade) with the marjoram or sage. Put into a
pan and fry gently until the fat runs. Drain off surplus fat.
Stir the purée and stock into the meat, cover and simmer for
1 hour, stirring occasionally and seasoning to taste. Cook the
lasagne in boiling salted water for 10 minutes and drain well.

Grate the Cheddar cheese (grating disc). Mix the butter,
flour and milk for 5 minutes (metal or plastic blade). Pour
into a saucepan and bring to the boil. Reduce heat and cook
for 2 minutes, stirring well. Cool for 5 minutes. Put into
the mixer bowl and add the egg yolk, nutmeg, cream, salt
and pepper. Mix for 5 seconds. Add half the cheese and mix
for 5 seconds. Grease an ovenproof dish and put in half the
meat mixture. Cover with half the lasagne and then half the
cheese sauce. Put in the remaining meat and lasagne. Cover
with the remaining cheese sauce and sprinkle with the
remaining grated cheese. Bake at 180°C/350°F/Gas Mark
4 for 35 minutes until golden-brown. Serve hot with a side
salad.

Make as above, but mince the beef with the coarse screen
of mincing attachment of a mixer. Chop the onion and herbs
finely in a blender. Grate the cheese with the grating
attachment of a mixer, or chop finely in a blender. Mix the
butter, flour and milk in a blender.

Liver Crumb Casserole

450g/1lb lamb's or pig's
    liver
25g/1oz plain flour
50g/2oz butter
2 onions
salt and pepper
225g/8oz day-old white bread
2 large sprigs parsley
300ml/½ pint stock

Cut the liver into thin slices and toss in the flour. Brown
lightly in the butter. Skin the onions and chop them coarsely
(metal blade). Cook in the butter until soft and golden.
Grease a casserole and arrange the liver and onions in layers,
sprinkling each onion layer with salt and pepper. Discard
the crusts and make the bread into crumbs (metal blade).
Chop the parsley finely (metal blade) and mix with the
crumbs. Sprinkle this mixture on top of the onions and pour
on the stock. Cover and cook at 180°C/350°F/Gas Mark 4
for 45 minutes. Remove the lid and continue cooking for 15
minutes to brown the crumbs. Serve with a green salad or
vegetables.

(CONTINUES)

Make as in the main method on page 53, but chop the onions in a blender. Prepare the breadcrumbs and parsley in a blender.

Pineapple Glazed Chicken

1·4kg/3lb chicken
1 large onion
75g/3oz butter
175g/6oz day-old white bread
50g/2oz walnut halves
4 canned pineapple rings
50g/2oz seedless raisins
2·5ml/$\frac{1}{2}$ teaspoon grated lemon rind
salt and pepper
90ml/6 tablespoons pineapple syrup from can

Remove the giblets from the chicken. Keep the liver for pâté or an omelet. Cook the remaining giblets in water to make stock. Skin the onion and chop finely (metal blade). Melt half the butter and cook the onion over low heat for 5 minutes until soft and golden. Discard the crusts and make the bread into crumbs (metal blade). Put into a bowl with the onion. Chop the walnuts finely (metal blade) and put into the bowl. Chop the pineapple coarsely (metal blade) and add to the bowl. Stir in the raisins, lemon rind, salt and pepper. Moisten with 30ml/2 tablespoons pineapple syrup and use to stuff the bird. Put into a roasting tin and spread with the remaining butter. Roast at 180°C/350°F/Gas Mark 4 for 1 hour. Pour on the remaining syrup and continue cooking for 15 minutes. Baste the chicken with the pan juices and continue cooking for 15 minutes. Lift the chicken on to a a serving dish. Add 150ml/$\frac{1}{4}$ pint giblet stock to the pan juices, heat and serve separately as gravy.

Make as above, but chop the onion in a blender. Prepare the breadcrumbs in a blender, and also the walnuts and pineapple.

Pizza

225g/8oz once-risen bread dough (page 107)
a little olive oil
350g/12oz Mozzarella or Cheddar cheese
450g/1lb tomatoes
5ml/1 teaspoon chopped fresh marjoram, thyme or basil
pepper
75g/3oz anchovy fillets
black olives

The bread dough should have risen until double in size. Turn on to a board and flatten into a long strip. Brush with a little oil and roll up like a Swiss roll. Repeat this process 3 times. Divide the dough into 4 pieces and roll each piece to a flat circle 18cm/7in across. Oil 4 flat tins (or a baking sheet), and put the dough in them. Brush the surface with olive oil. Cut the cheese in thin slices or grate (grating disc) and arrange half on the surface of the dough. Skin the tomatoes by dipping them in boiling water. Slice them and put on top of the cheese, then cover with the remaining cheese. Sprinkle with the herbs and pepper. Drain the anchovy fillets and arrange in a lattice on each pizza. Garnish with olives and

(CONTINUES)

sprinkle with a little olive oil. Bake at 230°C/450°F/Gas Mark 8 for 25 minutes.

Make as above, but grate the cheese with the grating attachment of a mixer, or chop finely in a blender. Chop any additional ingredients in a blender, or slice with the slicing attachment of a mixer.

Pizza Francescana
Cover the dough with 100g/4oz thinly sliced Bel Paese cheese, 225g/8oz chopped cooked ham, 100g/4oz chopped mushrooms and 225g/8oz sliced tomatoes. Season well, sprinkle with oil and bake as above.

Pizza San Remo
Prepare the dough as above. Chop 450g/1lb onions coarsely and cook in 50g/2oz butter for 15 minutes. Season to taste and spread on the dough. Drain a can of sardines and place the fish on top. Garnish with black olives and bake as above.

Pizza Sorrento
Prepare the pizza as above but omit the anchovy fillets and olives from the topping. Instead, arrange 100g/4oz sliced salami and 1 chopped green pepper on top of the tomatoes and cheese. Sprinkle with a little olive oil and bake as above.

Plain Omelet

2 eggs
30ml/2 tablespoons water
salt and pepper
butter for frying

Put the eggs, water and seasoning in the blender and blend until well mixed. Melt a knob of butter in a very hot omelet pan and pour in the mixture. Lower the heat and loosen the bottom of the omelet with a palette knife to allow the uncooked mixture to run underneath. As soon as it is set, put in the filling, fold and serve on a hot plate.

Fillings may be grated cheese, cooked vegetables, mushrooms, ham, asparagus, or creamed poultry, kidneys or fish.

Make as above, using the metal or plastic blade to mix the eggs, water and seasoning. Chop the filling ingredients with the metal blade to required fineness.

Pork Olives

4 thin slices lean pork
1 large onion
4 sage leaves
25g/1oz butter
100g/4oz day-old white bread
1 lemon
1 egg
salt and pepper
15g/½oz plain flour
300ml/½ pint stock

Beat the pieces of pork very flat with a rolling-pin. Skin the onion and chop finely with the sage leaves (metal blade). Melt the butter in a pan and cook the onion and sage for 5 minutes over low heat, stirring well. Lift out of the fat and put into a mixing bowl. Discard the crusts and make the bread into crumbs (metal blade). Add to the onion. Cut the lemon in half and cut one half into quarters for garnishing. Grate the rind from the other half and squeeze out the juice. Add the rind and juice to the breadcrumbs with the egg, salt and pepper. Mix well and divide the stuffing between the pieces of pork. Roll up and tie lightly with cotton. Dust the pork rolls with the flour and brown on all sides in the fat left in the pan. Add the stock, cover and simmer for 1½ hours. Remove the cotton from the meat. Put into a serving dish, pour over the pan juices and garnish with lemon wedges.

Make as above, but chop the onion and sage leaves in a blender. Prepare the breadcrumbs in a blender. Squeeze out the lemon juice with a juice extractor attachment, if available.

Portuguese Cod

4 cod steaks
100g/4oz streaky bacon,
    without rinds
1 large onion
1 green pepper
15ml/1 tablespoon oil
450g/1lb canned tomatoes
15ml/1 tablespoon
    concentrated tomato purée
2·5ml/½ teaspoon dried mixed
    herbs
salt and pepper
1 large sprig of parsley

Grill the cod steaks and put them in a greased ovenproof dish. Chop the bacon coarsely (metal blade). Skin the onion and chop finely (metal blade). Remove the stem and seeds from the pepper and chop coarsely (metal blade). Heat the oil in a pan and cook the bacon, onion and pepper for 5 minutes until soft and golden. Add the tomatoes and their juice, the tomato purée, herbs, salt and pepper. Cover and simmer for 10 minutes. Pour over the cod and bake at 160°C/325°F/Gas Mark 3 for 20 minutes. Chop the parsley finely (metal blade) and sprinkle on top just before serving.

Make as above, but chop the bacon and onion in a blender. Chop the pepper in a blender.

Quiche Lorraine

225g/8oz prepared shortcrust
    pastry (page 122)
1 medium onion
50g/2oz streaky bacon,
    without rinds
25g/1oz butter
2 eggs and 2 egg yolks
200ml/7fl oz creamy milk
pepper
100g/4oz cheese

Line a 20cm/8in flan ring or dish with the pastry. Skin the onion and cut it in pieces. Cut the bacon in pieces. Chop finely with the onion in the blender, and cook until soft in the butter. Put into the bottom of the flan. Put the eggs, egg yolks, milk and pepper in the blender, together with the cheese cut in small pieces. Blend so that the eggs and milk are well mixed together. Pour into the flan case. Bake at 190°C/375°F/Gas Mark 5 for 35 minutes. Serve hot or cold.

Make as above, chopping the bacon and onion with the metal blade. Mix the eggs, egg yolks, milk, pepper and cheese with the metal blade until the cheese is finely chopped.

Ratatouille Flan

225g/8oz prepared shortcrust
    pastry (page 122)
100g/4oz aubergine
100g/4oz tomatoes
1 small onion
1 small green pepper
100g/4oz streaky bacon
50g/2oz butter
salt and pepper
100g/4oz Cheddar cheese

Roll out the pastry and use to line a 20cm/8in flan ring or tin. Cut the aubergine in pieces. Skin the tomatoes and remove the pips. Skin the onion and cut in pieces, and remove the seeds from the green pepper. Cut the bacon in pieces. Put the vegetables and bacon in the blender and blend until roughly chopped. Cook gently in the butter until the vegetables are soft but not coloured. Season with salt and pepper and leave until cold. Put into the pastry case. Cut the cheese in pieces and blend in small quantities until finely chopped. Bake the filled flan at 200°C/400°F/Gas Mark 6 for 30 minutes. Spread the cheese on top of the vegetables and continue baking for 15 minutes until the cheese has melted and is golden-brown. Serve hot.

Make as above, chopping the bacon and vegetables with the metal blade. Chop the cheese finely with the metal blade.

Roast Lamb with Apricot Stuffing

100g/4oz dried apricots
225g/8oz day-old white bread
2 celery sticks
50g/2oz melted butter
salt and pepper
1·4kg/3lb boned shoulder of
     lamb
3 sprigs rosemary

Cover the apricots with water, bring to the boil and simmer for 5 minutes. Drain, reserving the liquid. Discard crusts and cut the bread into pieces. Make into breadcrumbs (metal blade). Keep the breadcrumbs on one side. Wash and trim the celery. Cool the apricots for 10 minutes and put into the mixer bowl with the pieces of celery. Chop coarsely (metal blade). Mix the apricots and celery with the reserved liquid, breadcrumbs, butter and seasoning. Stuff the lamb and tie the meat carefully so that the stuffing cannot escape. Put the joint into a roasting tin and place a rosemary sprig on top. Roast at 190°C/375°F/Gas Mark 5 for 2 hours, basting occasionally with the pan juices. Before serving, replace the rosemary with fresh sprigs. As the stuffing is richly flavoured, serve with plainly boiled potatoes rather than roast potatoes.

Make as above, but prepare the breadcrumbs in a blender. Chop the apricots and celery in a blender.

Salmon Mousse

450g/1lb canned pink salmon
25g/1oz butter
25g/1oz plain flour
300ml/½ pint milk
salt and pepper
45ml/3 tablespoons tomato
     ketchup
5ml/1 teaspoon anchovy
     essence
2·5ml/½ teaspoon lemon juice
15g/½oz gelatine
30ml/2 tablespoons water
150ml/¼ pint double cream
2 egg whites

Prepare a 15cm/6in soufflé dish by tying a band of paper or foil round the outside so that it comes about 5cm/2in above the top of the dish. Drain the salmon and remove skin and bones. Mash the salmon lightly with a fork. Melt the butter, stir in the flour and cook gently for 1 minute. Add the milk and bring to the boil, stirring all the time. Simmer for 3 minutes and season with salt and pepper. Cool slightly and put into the blender with the salmon, tomato ketchup, anchovy essence and lemon juice. Stir the gelatine into the water and heat in a bowl over hot water until the gelatine is syrupy. Add to the blender and blend until smooth and creamy. Whip the cream to soft peaks and fold into the salmon mixture. Whisk the egg whites to stiff peaks, fold in the salmon mixture and pour into the soufflé dish. Leave in a cold place until set, and remove the paper collar carefully. Garnish with thin slices of cucumber and stuffed olives.

Make as above, mixing the sauce, salmon, tomato ketchup, anchovy essence, lemon juice and gelatine mixture with the plastic blade.

Roast Lamb with Apricot Stuffing

Savoury Soufflés

50g/2oz plain flour
300ml/½ pint milk
3 size 1-2 eggs, separated
75g/3oz butter
salt and pepper

Put the flour, milk and egg yolks into the blender and blend on low speed until smooth. Melt the butter and stir in the milk mixture, cooking gently and stirring well until smooth and thick. Remove from the heat. Whisk the egg whites to stiff peaks and fold into the sauce. Grease a 1·2 litre/2 pint soufflé dish, fill with the mixture and bake at 190°C/375°F/ Gas Mark 5 for 45 minutes. Serve and eat at once.

Make as above, mixing the flour, milk and egg yolks with the plastic blade. When making additions, add the sauce to flavouring ingredients, process with the metal blade until the ingredients are finely chopped.

Flavourings

Asparagus
Add 175g/6oz cooked or canned asparagus to the cooked sauce, and blend until the asparagus is just chopped before folding in the egg whites.

Cheese
Add 100g/4oz diced Cheddar cheese to milk mixture in the blender with 2·5ml/½ teaspoon mustard powder before cooking the sauce.

Chicken
Add 100g/4oz cooked chicken, a small piece of lemon rind and 1 teaspoon parsley to the cooked sauce, and blend until the chicken is just chopped before folding in the egg whites.

Crab
Add 100g/4oz crabmeat to the sauce, and blend until just mixed before folding in the egg whites.

Danish
Add 175g/6oz chopped cooked bacon, 25g/1oz cheese and a little made mustard to the cooked sauce, and blend until the bacon is finely chopped before folding in the egg whites.

Fish
Add 100g/4oz cooked fish to the sauce, and blend until just mixed before folding in the egg whites. Smoked haddock or kipper are particularly good.

Mushroom
Cook 175g/6oz mushrooms in a little butter, and blend with the cooked sauce until finely chopped before folding in the egg whites.

Seafood
Add 100g/4oz cooked prawns or shrimps and a squeeze of lemon juice to the sauce, and blend until coarsely chopped before folding in the egg whites.

Tomato
Add 60ml/4 tablespoons concentrated tomato purée to the milk mixture before cooking the sauce.

Savoury Stuffed Pancakes

300ml/½ pint milk
1 egg
a pinch of salt
100g/4oz plain flour

Filling
175g/6oz cooked chicken
1 small onion
100g/4oz button mushrooms
25g/1oz butter
450ml/¾ pint white sauce
   (page 73)
salt and pepper
50g/2oz Cheddar cheese

Mix the milk, egg and salt for 5 seconds (metal or plastic blade). Tip in the flour and mix until smooth and creamy. Grease an 18cm/7in frying pan lightly and fry 8 thin pancakes. Keep warm.

To make the filling, chop the chicken finely (metal blade). Keep on one side. Skin the onion, wipe the mushrooms and chop finely (metal blade). Cook the onion and mushroom mixture in the butter until just soft and golden. Stir in the chicken and mix well. Add 150ml/¼ pint white sauce, mix well and season to taste. Divide this mixture between the pancakes and roll them up. Arrange in a fireproof dish. Chop the cheese (metal blade) and add to the remaining white sauce, stirring until just melted. Spoon over the pancakes. Put under a hot grill until the sauce is bubbling and golden.

Make as above, but prepare the batter in a blender or with a mixer. When making the filling, chop the chicken finely in a blender. Chop the onion and mushrooms in a blender.

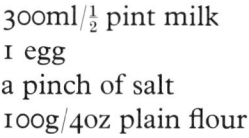

Sicilian Chicken

4 chicken joints
salt and pepper
60ml/4 tablespoons olive oil
10ml/2 teaspoons marjoram
45ml/3 tablespoons lemon
 juice
1 garlic clove
5ml/1 teaspoon parsley

Wipe the chicken joints and sprinkle them with salt and pepper. Put the oil, marjoram, lemon juice, chopped garlic and parsley into the blender and blend until the herbs are finely chopped. Brush this mixture generously on the chicken pieces on both sides. Put into a grill pan about 15cm/6in from the heat and grill for about 20 minutes on each side until brown and tender, turning once only, and sometimes brushing with the mixture. Heat any remaining sauce and pour over the hot chicken to serve. This is good with a green salad or it can be served with fried potatoes and peas or French beans.

Make as above, chopping the herbs and garlic with the metal blade.

A Savoury Soufflé

Savoury Stuffed Pancakes (page 61)

Spanish Omelet

2 potatoes
1 small red pepper
1 small onion
4 mushrooms
30ml/2 tablespoons cooking
    oil
50g/2oz cooked peas
4 eggs
30ml/2 tablespoons water
salt and pepper
25g/1oz butter
1 sprig of parsley

Peel the potatoes and chip them (chipping disc). Put into cold water, bring to the boil for 5 minutes. Drain well. Cut the pepper in half and remove the stem and seeds. Skin the onion and wipe the mushrooms. Chop the pepper, onion and mushrooms coarsely (metal blade). Heat the oil in a heavy-based frying pan and cook the potato pieces over gentle heat until golden and soft. Add the pepper, onion and mushrooms and stir together over low heat until soft but not coloured. Stir in the peas. While the vegetables are cooking, mix the eggs with the water, salt and pepper until just blended (plastic blade). Add the butter to the pan and when it has just melted, pour in the eggs. Cook gently, stirring and lifting the egg mixture from the bottom of the pan. When the eggs are set but still creamy, the omelet is ready. Chop the parsley (metal blade). Sprinkle over the omelet. Serve in slices.

Make as above, but slice the potatoes with the slicing attachment of a mixer, or chop them in a blender. Chop the pepper, onion and mushrooms in a blender. Make the egg mixture in a blender while the vegetables are cooking.

Stuffed Baked Marrow

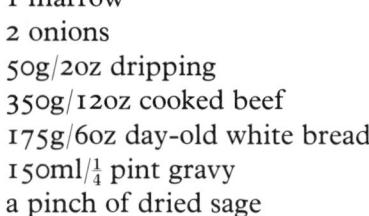

1 marrow
2 onions
50g/2oz dripping
350g/12oz cooked beef
175g/6oz day-old white bread
150ml/¼ pint gravy
a pinch of dried sage
salt and pepper

Trim the ends from the marrow. Peel it and cut through lengthways to remove the top third. Scoop out the seeds and pith. Skin the onions and chop them finely in a blender. Fry in a little of the dripping until soft and golden. Mince the cooked meat with the coarse screen of the mincing attachment. Stir in the onion and cook for 5 minutes. Discard the crusts, make the bread into crumbs in a blender and mix with the onions and the meat. Remove from the heat and stir in the gravy, sage, salt and pepper. Fill the marrow and replace the lid. Spread the remaining dripping on top. Bake at 200°C/400°F/Gas Mark 6 for 1 hour. Serve in slices with plenty of gravy.

Make as above, chopping the onions with the metal blade. Cut the meat into pieces and chop finely with the metal blade. Prepare the breadcrumbs with the metal blade.

Stuffed Liver

350g/12oz lamb's or pig's
    liver
50g/2oz fresh white bread
1 small onion
1 sprig parsley
1 small egg
2·5ml/½ teaspoon
    Worcestershire sauce
6 rashers streaky bacon
300ml/½ pint stock

Cut the liver in thin slices and put into a greased ovenproof dish. Put the bread into the blender and blend into crumbs. Put the breadcrumbs into a bowl. Skin the onion, cut it into pieces and put into the blender with the parsley, egg and Worcestershire sauce. Cover and blend until the parsley is chopped finely. Add this mixture to the breadcrumbs and mix well. Put this stuffing on top of the liver slices, and cover with bacon rashers. Pour on the stock. Bake at 180°C/350°F/Gas Mark 4 for 40 minutes.

Make as above, preparing the breadcrumbs with the metal blade. Chop the onion with the parsley, egg and sauce with the metal blade.

Stuffed Peppers in Tomato Sauce

4 green peppers
1 small onion
1 garlic clove
225g/8oz chuck steak
2 rashers streaky bacon,
    without rinds
225g/8oz chicken livers
15ml/1 tablespoon oil
salt and pepper

Tomato Sauce
1 onion
25g/1oz butter
25g/1oz plain flour
400g/14oz canned tomatoes
15ml/1 tablespoon
    concentrated tomato purée
5ml/1 teaspoon sugar
a pinch of dried mixed herbs
salt and pepper

Bring to the boil a pan of salted water. Remove the lids from the peppers and set aside. Discard the seeds and put the peppers into the boiling water. Boil for 5 minutes, and drain thoroughly. Put the peppers into a greased ovenproof dish. Skin the onion and garlic and chop coarsely in a blender. Cut the beef into cubes. Mince the bacon, beef and chicken livers with the fine screen of the mincing attachment and add to the onion. Heat the oil in a pan and cook the meat mixture until lightly browned, stirring well. Season to taste and spoon the mixture into the peppers. Replace the lids lightly on the peppers.

To make the sauce, skin the onion and chop it finely in a blender. Melt the butter in a pan and fry the onion until soft and golden. Return to the blender with the remaining ingredients, and mix until smooth. Put through a sieve to remove the pips. Put into a pan, bring to the boil and simmer for 5 minutes, stirring all the time. Adjust the seasoning if necessary. Pour the sauce over the peppers, cover with a lid or foil and bake at 180°C/350°F/Gas Mark 4 for 40 minutes. These peppers are delicious served cold as a first course, but they are also good with an accompaniment of savoury rice.

Make as above, chopping the onion and garlic with the metal blade. Add the bacon, beef and chicken livers to the onion

(CONTINUES)

and continue pressing until the beef is finely chopped. When making the sauce, chop the onion with the metal blade. Blend the sauce ingredients together with the plastic blade.

Stuffed Plaice in Shrimp Sauce

4 small plaice
1 small onion
50g/2oz button mushrooms
25g/1oz butter
75g/3oz day-old white bread
salt and pepper

Sauce
25g/1oz butter
25g/1oz plain flour
450ml/¾ pint milk
1 lemon
salt and pepper
100g/4oz peeled shrimps or
  prawns
1 sprig of parsley

Make a cut down the centre of one side of each fish. Skin the onion and chop finely (metal blade). Wipe the mushrooms and chop (metal blade). Melt the butter and cook the onion and mushrooms gently, stirring well, for 5 minutes. Discard the crusts and make the bread into fine crumbs (metal blade). Add the onion mixture to the crumbs and season well. Insert this stuffing into the cuts in the fish. Grease an ovenproof dish and place the fish in it. Bake at 200°C/400°F/Gas Mark 6 for 20 minutes.

Make the sauce by blending the butter, flour and milk. Heat and stir over low heat until the sauce is thick and creamy. Grate the lemon rind and keep on one side. Squeeze out the juice and add to the sauce. Season to taste. Chop the shrimps or prawns coarsely (metal blade). Add to the sauce and heat through. Pour over the fish and continue baking for 15 minutes. Chop the parsley finely (metal blade) and mix with the grated lemon rind. Just before serving, sprinkle the parsley and lemon on to the fish.

Make as above, but chop the onion and mushrooms in a blender. Prepare the breadcrumbs in a blender.

Make the sauce in a blender and add the shrimps or prawns, blending until just chopped before re-heating.

Right Spanish Omelet (page 64)

Stuffed Tomatoes

4 large tomatoes
50g/2oz white bread
1 small onion
15ml/1 tablespoon parsley
50g/2oz melted butter
salt and pepper

Cut the tops of the tomatoes to form 'lids' and keep on one side. Scoop out the pulp from the tomatoes and put into a bowl, removing as many pips as possible. Break the bread into small pieces and make into breadcrumbs in the blender, adding the chopped onion and parsley during the final blending until the onion is finely chopped. Put into the bowl with the tomato pulp, and add melted butter and seasoning. Leave to stand for 10 minutes, then put into the tomato cases. Put back the 'lids'. Arrange in a lightly greased oven-proof dish and bake at 200°C/400°F/Gas Mark 6 for 15 minutes. Serve hot.

Make as above, preparing the breadcrumbs, onion and parsley with the metal blade. Chop any additional ingredients with the metal blade.

Cheese Tomatoes
Add 50g/2oz cheese to final blending.

Ham Tomatoes
Add 50g/2oz finely chopped cooked ham and $2.5ml/\frac{1}{2}$ teaspoon made mustard.

Lamb Tomatoes
Add 50g/2oz finely chopped lean lamb and $2.5ml/\frac{1}{2}$ teaspoon mixed herbs.

Prawn Tomatoes
Substitute 50g/2oz peeled prawns for the onion.

Sweet and Sour Pork

675g/1½lb lean pork
juice of ½ lemon
1 egg
100g/4oz plain flour
150ml/¼ pint milk
salt and pepper
fat for deep frying
sweet and sour sauce (page 82)

Cut the pork into 2.5cm/1in cubes and leave in a bowl with the lemon juice for 30 minutes. Put the egg, flour, milk and seasoning into the blender and blend until creamy and smooth. Drain the pork pieces, dip in the batter and fry until golden-brown and crisp. Drain on kitchen paper and serve with Sweet and Sour Sauce.

Make as above, preparing the batter with the plastic blade.

Sweet and Sour Red Cabbage

900g/2lb red cabbage
2 small onions
1 eating apple
15g/½oz butter
15ml/1 tablespoon dark soft
    brown sugar
15ml/1 tablespoon vinegar
300ml/½ pint dry cider
salt and pepper

Remove outer leaves from the cabbage and take out the hard stem. Wash and shred the cabbage (slicing disc). Skin the onions and chop finely (metal blade). Peel and core the apple and chop coarsely (metal blade). Melt the butter in a pan and cook the onion for 5 minutes over low heat, stirring well. Add the sugar and vinegar and put in the cabbage. Stir well and add the cider, salt and pepper. Cover and simmer for 1 hour. Stir in the apple pieces and continue cooking for 1 hour. If preferred, the cabbage can be cooked in the oven at 160°C/325°F/Gas Mark 3 for 2 hours. It is particularly good with sausages, pork or duck.

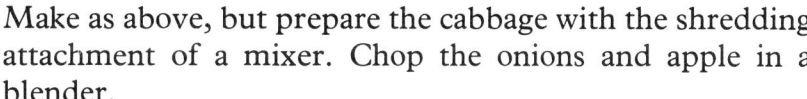

Make as above, but prepare the cabbage with the shredding attachment of a mixer. Chop the onions and apple in a blender.

Swiss Potato Cake

900g/2lb potatoes
1 onion
75g/3oz butter
50g/2oz Gruyère cheese
salt and pepper

Wash the potatoes and parboil them in their skins for 10 minutes. Cool and peel. Cut into large pieces and grate (grating disc). Skin the onion and chop finely (metal blade). Melt half the butter in a pan and cook the onion for 5 minutes until soft. Add the remaining butter and then the potatoes. Grate the cheese (grating disc) and add to the mixture. Season and stir well. Press the mixture down firmly with a palette knife and cook for about 10 minutes until golden-brown underneath. Turn the potato cake over carefully with a fish slice and continue cooking for 10 minutes. Serve cut into wedges.

Make as above, but prepare the potatoes with the grating attachment of a mixer. Chop the onion finely in a blender. Chop the cheese finely in a blender.

Veal and Ham Pie

450g/1lb prepared hot water
   crust pastry (page 116)
450g/1lb pie veal
100g/4oz raw ham or lean
   bacon
a pinch of dried thyme
salt and pepper
1 hard-boiled egg
300ml/½ pint jellied stock
beaten egg for glazing

Use three-quarters of the pastry to line a 450g/1lb loaf tin. (If possible, use a tin with sides that unclip, which makes removal much easier.) Cut the veal and ham or bacon into pieces and mince with the coarse screen of the mincing attachment. Mix with the thyme, salt and pepper. Put half the meat mixture into the pastry case and place the egg in the centre. Cover with the remaining meat. Add 2 tablespoons stock. Cover with a lid of the remaining pastry and decorate with any trimmings. Make a small hole in the centre of the lid. Brush with beaten egg. Bake at 220°C/425°F/Gas Mark 7 for 30 minutes. Reduce the heat to 160°C/325°F/Gas Mark 3 and continue cooking for 1½ hours. Cover the pastry with greaseproof paper or foil if it browns too quickly. Remove from the oven and leave in the tin. After 45 minutes, put a small funnel into the hole in the lid. Heat the stock until it is just liquid. Spoon into the pie through the funnel. Leave until completely cold before removing from the tin.

Make as above, chopping the veal, ham and bacon coarsely with the metal blade.

Waldorf Salad

4 red-skinned eating apples
10ml/2 teaspoons lemon juice
½ cucumber
3 celery sticks
75g/3oz walnut halves
2 sprigs parsley
150ml/¼ pint mayonnaise
crisp lettuce leaves
watercress sprigs

Wipe and core the apples but do not peel them. Cut into quarters and chop coarsely (metal blade). Put into a bowl and sprinkle with lemon juice. Peel the cucumber and chop coarsely (metal blade). Wash and trim the celery and chop coarsely with the walnuts (metal blade). Mix the cucumber, celery and walnuts with the apples. Chop the parsley (metal blade) and add to the mixture. Stir in the mayonnaise until the pieces are well-coated. Arrange the lettuce leaves on a serving dish and pile the salad in the centre. Garnish with watercress sprigs.

Make as above, but chop the apples in a blender. Also chop the cucumber, celery, walnuts and parsley in a blender.

Yorkshire Pudding

300ml/½ pint milk
1 egg
2·5ml/½ teaspoon salt
100g/4oz plain flour

Put all the ingredients into the blender, putting in the flour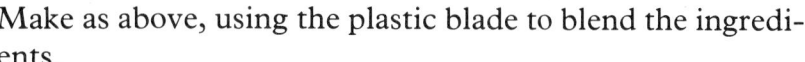
last, and blend until creamy. Pour 45ml/3 tablespoons fat
from the roasting joint into a shallow baking tin and heat
in the oven until smoking hot. Pour in the batter and bake
at 200°C/400°F/Gas Mark 6 for 30 minutes until brown and
risen.

Make as above, using the plastic blade to blend the ingredients.

Savoury Sauces and Stuffings

Barbecue Sauce

1 medium onion
25g/1oz butter
15g/½oz plain flour
10ml/2 teaspoons French
    mustard
2·5ml/½ teaspoon dry mustard
15ml/1 tablespoon
    Worcestershire sauce
5ml/1 teaspoon Tabasco sauce
15g/½oz brown sugar
5ml/1 teaspoon salt
15ml/1 tablespoon vinegar
250ml/8fl oz tomato juice

Skin the onion, cut it into pieces, and chop finely in the blender. Cook in the butter until golden. Stir in the flour and cook for 2 minutes. Put into the blender with the remaining ingredients, and blend until smooth. Bring to boiling point and then simmer for 5 minutes, stirring well.

Make as above, but chop the onion finely with the metal blade. Process the onion and flour mixture with the remaining ingredients until smooth, using the metal blade.

Basic Poultry Stuffing

1 small loaf day-old bread
1 medium onion
45ml/3 tablespoons parsley
15ml/1 tablespoon thyme
50g/2oz melted butter
salt and pepper
5ml/1 teaspoon lemon juice

Cut the bread into small pieces and blend in small quantities to make fine breadcrumbs. Put the crumbs into a bowl. Cut the onion in pieces and put into the blender with the remaining ingredients. Blend until the herbs are finely chopped. Pour on to the breadcrumbs and stir until well mixed. An egg may be added for a more solid stuffing. This is enough for a bird weighing 2kg/4lb.

Giblet Stuffing
The giblets of the bird can be cooked, and the liver, heart and meat from the neck added to the herbs and butter to be finely chopped before adding to the breadcrumbs.

Raisin and Nut Stuffing
Chop 100g/4oz walnut halves and 175g/6oz seedless raisins in the blender and add to the other ingredients. Use for poultry or pork.

(CONTINUES)

Make as above, but prepare the breadcrumbs with the metal blade and transfer to a bowl. Chop the onion and herbs finely with the metal blade before mixing with the breadcrumbs.

Giblet Stuffing
Chop the cooked giblets finely, using the metal blade.

Raisin and Nut Stuffing
Chop the walnuts and raisins coarsely, using the metal blade.

Basic White Sauce

25g/1oz melted butter
25g/1oz plain flour
300ml/½ pint milk
salt and white pepper

Mix the butter, flour and milk until smooth (plastic blade). Pour into a pan, bring to the boil and simmer for 3 minutes, stirring all the time. Season to taste. If a flavoured sauce is needed, prepare the additional ingredients in the processor before making the sauce.

Chop the additional ingredients in a blender and put into a bowl before making sauce. Blend the butter, flour and milk until smooth before cooking.

Cheese Sauce
Stir 75g/3oz grated or chopped cheese into the sauce just before serving.

Egg Sauce
Stir 2 chopped hard-boiled eggs into the cooked sauce.

Onion Sauce
Cook 1 finely chopped medium onion in the sauce. Flavour with a pinch of ground nutmeg.

Parsley Sauce
Stir 2 large chopped sprigs of parsley into the cooked sauce.

Shrimp Sauce
Add 75g/3oz peeled, finely chopped shrimps to the cooked sauce and season with a few drops of Tabasco sauce.

Basic Brown Sauce

2 rashers streaky bacon,
   without rinds
1 onion
1 celery stick
1 carrot
4 large mushrooms
30ml/2 tablespoons oil
25g/1oz plain flour
450ml/¾ pint beef stock
30ml/2 tablespoons
   concentrated tomato purée
1 bay leaf
1 sprig of parsley
salt and pepper

Chop the bacon finely (metal blade). Skin the onion and chop finely (metal blade). Chop the celery, carrot, mushrooms finely (metal blade). Heat the oil and stir in the bacon and vegetables. Stir over low heat until the onions are soft and golden. Add the flour and stir well for 2 minutes over low heat. Add the stock gradually and then the remaining ingredients. Bring to the boil, cover and simmer for 45 minutes. Take out the bay leaf and parsley. Blend the sauce until smooth. Return to the pan and simmer for 10 minutes. Use for meat dishes.

Make as above, but chop the bacon and vegetables finely in a blender.

Bread Sauce with Onion

1 small onion
300ml/½ pint milk
a pinch of ground cloves
100g/4oz day-old white bread
25g/1oz butter
salt and pepper
30ml/2 tablespoons single
   cream

Skin the onion and chop finely (metal blade). Put into a pan with the milk and cloves and bring slowly to boiling point. Leave it to stand in a warm place for 30 minutes. Discard the crusts and make the bread into crumbs (metal blade). Stir the crumbs into the milk and simmer for 5 minutes. Stir in the butter, salt, pepper and cream, and serve at once. This is more strongly flavoured than the usual bread sauce and is very good with chicken, game or sausages.

Make as above, but chop the onions finely in a blender. Make the breadcrumbs in a blender.

Chestnut Stuffing

450g/1lb chestnuts
milk
50g/2oz day-old bread
25g/1oz melted butter
10ml/2 teaspoons fresh mixed
    herbs
2 eggs
salt and pepper
a pinch of mustard powder

Split the chestnuts and boil them in water for 10 minutes. Remove and discard the skin and process the chestnuts until finely chopped (metal blade). Add just enough milk to cover, and cook until tender. Cut the bread into small pieces, add to the chestnuts with the butter, herbs, egg and seasoning, and process until well mixed (metal blade). Use for chicken or turkey, but double the quantity for a large turkey.

Make as above, but cook the chestnuts in a little milk before chopping them in a blender. Add the rest of the ingredients and blend until well mixed.

Chutney Sauce

45ml/3 tablespoons spicy
    bottled sauce
15ml/1 tablespoon
    concentrated tomato purée
150ml/¼ pint apple purée
2 eating apples
1 banana
15g/½oz shelled almonds
15g/½oz shelled walnuts
50g/2oz raisins

Put the bottled sauce, tomato purée and apple purée into the blender. Peel and core the apples and cut them in rough pieces. Cut the banana in pieces. Put into the blender with the nuts, and blend until the nuts are finely chopped. Mix with the raisins and serve hot or cold with meat, poultry or fish.

Make as above, chopping apples coarsely first with the metal  blade. Add the banana, sauce, tomato and apple purées and process until smooth, using the metal blade. Add the nuts and process only until the nuts are finely chopped, using the metal blade.

Cranberry Apple Sauce

450g/1lb cranberries
450g/1lb cooking apples
600ml/1 pint water
175g/6oz sugar

Put the cranberries and the peeled and cored apples into the blender in small quantities with the water and blend until finely chopped. Add the sugar and simmer over low heat until the fruit is soft. Return to the blender and blend until smooth. Serve with pork or turkey.

Make as above, but chop the cranberries and apples finely with the metal blade. Process the cooked fruit and liquid in small quantities until smooth, using the metal or plastic blade.

Curry Sauce

1 onion
15ml/1 tablespoon oil
25g/1oz plain flour
15g/½oz curry powder
5ml/1 teaspoon curry paste
450ml/¾ pint beef or chicken stock
1 eating apple
50g/2oz sultanas
10ml/2 teaspoons lemon juice
salt and pepper

Skin the onion and chop finely in a blender. Cook over low heat in the oil until soft and golden. Stir in the flour, curry powder and paste, and continue cooking for 3 minutes. Add the stock and simmer over low heat for 10 minutes. Peel and core the apple and chop finely in a blender. Add to the sauce with the sultanas, lemon juice and seasoning. Simmer for 10 minutes. If a smooth sauce is preferred, blend before adding the sultanas and seasonings. Serve with cooked meat, poultry, fish, seafood or eggs.

Make as above, but chop the onion finely with the metal blade. Chop the apple finely with the metal blade.

Gooseberry Sauce

225g/8oz green gooseberries
30ml/2 tablespoons water
25g/1oz butter
25g/1oz sugar
a pinch of ground allspice

Top and tail the gooseberries. Chop them finely (metal blade). Put into a pan with the water and simmer for 5 minutes. Cool slightly. Mix with the butter, sugar and spice until smooth (plastic blade). Return to a clean pan and re-heat. Serve with mackerel or other oily fish.

Make as above, but chop the gooseberries with the water in a blender. Put the cooked berries into a blender with the butter, sugar and spice and blend until smooth before re-heating.

Hollandaise Sauce

3 egg yolks
15ml/1 tablespoon lemon
juice
15ml/1 tablespoon warm
water
salt and white pepper
100g/4oz unsalted butter

Mix the egg yolks, lemon juice, water, salt and pepper until just blended (plastic blade). Melt the butter without browning. With the machine running, pour the butter slowly through the feeder tube until completely mixed in and the sauce is thick. Serve immediately with fish, asparagus, artichokes or other vegetables.

Make as above, but blend the ingredients on low speed for 5 seconds before adding the warm butter gently through the lid of a blender. Continue blending until the sauce has thickened, switch off immediately.

Aurora Sauce
Fold 45ml/3 tablespoons mayonnaise and 150ml/$\frac{1}{4}$ pint whipped cream into the Hollandaise sauce, and serve with cold chicken or fish.

Maltaise Sauce
Stir in 5ml/1 teaspoon grated orange rind and 15ml/1 tablespoon orange juice and serve with vegetables.

Mousseline Sauce
Before preparing Hollandaise Sauce, whip 150ml/$\frac{1}{4}$ pint double cream to soft peaks and keep on one side. Prepare the sauce and fold in the cream. Serve with fish, vegetables or eggs.

Horseradish Cream Sauce

150ml/$\frac{1}{4}$ pint double cream
15ml/1 tablespoon lemon
juice
5ml/1 teaspoon horseradish
sauce
10ml/2 teaspoons
Worcestershire sauce
2 spring onions

Put cream, lemon juice, horseradish sauce and Worcestershire sauce into the blender. Cut the white part and a little of the green of the onions into pieces and add to the blender. Blend until the onions are very finely chopped. Chill and serve with steak, roast beef, hamburgers or jacket potatoes.

Make as above, but blend the ingredients with the metal blade until finely chopped.

Mayonnaise tastes equally delicious whether made with a mixer, blender or food processor

Mixer Mayonnaise

2 egg yolks
2·5ml/½ teaspoon salt
2·5ml/½ teaspoon mustard
    powder
1·25ml/¼ teaspoon pepper
300ml/½ pint olive oil
15ml/1 tablespoon lemon
    juice or vinegar

Put the egg yolks with salt, mustard and pepper into the mixer bowl and whisk on maximum speed for 10 seconds. Drop in the olive oil very slowly, with the mixer running, until nearly all the oil has been completely absorbed. Add the lemon juice or vinegar and continue whisking until all the oil has been absorbed.

Blender Mayonnaise

1 size 3-4 egg
15ml/1 tablespoon vinegar or
    lemon juice
2·5ml/½ teaspoon salt
5ml/1 teaspoon sugar
1·25ml/¼ teaspoon dry
    mustard
1·25ml/¼ teaspoon pepper
300ml/½ pint salad oil

Put the egg, vinegar or lemon juice, salt, sugar, mustard and pepper into the blender. Cover and blend on medium speed for 5 seconds. Start to pour the oil gently through the centre section of the cover while the blender is running. Continue blending for about 1 minute until the oil has been incorporated. It may be necessary to stop the blender and scrape down the sides with a spatula. This gives a creamy mixture, but if a thicker mayonnaise is preferred, use two egg yolks instead of the whole egg.

Processor Mayonnaise

1 egg and 1 egg yolk
2·5ml/½ teaspoon mustard
    powder
salt and white pepper
300ml/½ pint oil
15ml/1 tablespoon wine
    vinegar or lemon juice

Mix the egg, egg yolk, mustard, salt and pepper until smooth (metal blade). With the machine running pour half the oil slowly through the feeder tube (metal blade). Switch off the machine to change blades. Add the remaining oil through the feeder tube and mix until the mayonnaise is thick (plastic blade). Add vinegar or lemon juice and process until mixed.

Variations to Mixer, Blender, Processor Mayonnaise

Cucumber Mayonnaise
Cut up ¼ cucumber (including the skin) and blend with 1 slice of onion, 10ml/2 teaspoons mild made mustard, salt and pepper until the cucumber is finely chopped. Add 45ml/3 tablespoons mayonnaise and blend until just mixed. Serve with fish, poultry or ham.

(CONTINUES)

Curry Mayonnaise

Add 15ml/1 tablespoon tomato purée, 15ml/1 tablespoon curry paste, 5ml/1 teaspoon lemon juice and 30ml/2 tablespoons double cream to the mayonnaise. Blend until smooth.

Green Mayonnaise

Chop 1 garlic clove, 15ml/1 tablespoon fresh dill, 15ml/1 tablespoon fresh chives and 15ml/1 tablespoon fresh parsley and add to the mayonnaise. Use for tomatoes, cucumbers or fish.

Green Goddess Mayonnaise

Use tarragon vinegar for the mayonnaise. Chop 1 garlic clove, 2 anchovy fillets, 3 spring onions (including green tops) and 30ml/2 tablespoons parsley and add to the mayonnaise. Use for seafood.

Niçoise Mayonnaise

Add 1 chopped garlic clove and 2·5ml/½ teaspoon chopped tarragon with 30ml/2 tablespoons concentrated tomato purée to the mayonnaise. Blend until smooth.

Tomato Mayonnaise

Cut up 1 small green pepper, and blend with 30ml/2 tablespoons tomato purée, 5ml/1 teaspoon tarragon and 15ml/1 tablespoon chives, before adding to the mayonnaise. Use for seafood.

Tartare Sauce

1 recipe quantity mayonnaise
  (page 79)
8 sprigs parsley
6 gherkins
6 stuffed olives
2 pickled onions
10ml/2 teaspoons capers

Make the mayonnaise as in previous recipes and, during the last stage of thickening, add the other ingredients until coarsely chopped. Serve with fish.

Sage and Onion Stuffing

2 large onions
300ml/½ pint water
50g/2oz day-old bread
10ml/2 teaspoons fresh sage
 leaves
25g/1oz melted butter
salt and pepper

Cut the onions in pieces and put into the blender with the water. Blend until the onions are coarsely chopped. Simmer for 20 minutes, and drain off the cooking liquid, but keep it in reserve. Break the bread into small pieces and blend in small quantities with the sage until the bread forms fine breadcrumbs. Mix the crumbs, sage, melted butter, seasoning, onions and enough cooking liquid to give a moist texture. Use for duck, goose or pork, or for hearts.

Make as above, but chop the onions coarsely, using the metal blade. Make breadcrumbs and chop sage, using the metal blade.

Sausage Stuffing

50g/2oz streaky bacon,
 without rinds
liver from poultry
1 onion
25g/1oz butter
1 egg
50g/2oz fresh white bread
450g/1lb pork sausage-meat
10ml/2 teaspoons fresh mixed
 herbs
stock
salt and pepper

Chop the bacon and liver finely (metal blade). Chop the onion finely (metal blade). Fry the bacon and liver in the butter until soft but not coloured. Make crumbs from the bread (metal blade). Mix all the ingredients, including the pan juices, and enough stock to cover, with the sausage-meat in the processor bowl. Use for chicken or turkey.

Make as above, but cut up the bacon and liver in small pieces. When cooked, put into a blender with the rest of the ingredients and blend until the meat is finely chopped.

Spaghetti Sauce

1 onion
1 garlic clove
30ml/2 tablespoons oil
1 carrot
675g/1½lb chuck steak
1 chicken liver
100g/4oz button mushrooms
25g/1oz plain flour
225g/8oz canned tomatoes
300ml/½ pint beef stock
60ml/4 tablespoons red wine

Skin the onion and garlic and chop finely (metal blade). Heat the oil in a pan and stir in the onion and garlic until soft and golden. Peel the carrot and chop finely (metal blade). Add to the onion and cook for 3 minutes. Cut the steak and liver into pieces and chop finely (metal blade). Add to the pan and continue cooking until lightly browned. Wipe the mushrooms and chop finely (metal blade). Add to the pan and cook for 2 minutes. Drain off surplus fat from the pan. Work in the flour and cook for 1 minute. Drain the tomatoes and add the juice to the pan. Cut tomatoes and remove seeds. Chop

(CONTINUES)

60ml/4 tablespoons
    concentrated tomato purée
2·5ml/½ teaspoon dried mixed
    herbs
salt and pepper

the flesh finely (metal blade) and add to the pan. Stir in the remaining ingredients and bring to the boil. Cover, lower the heat and simmer for 1 hour. Serve with any pasta.

Make as above, but chop the vegetables finely in a blender. Mince the steak and chicken liver through the fine screen of the mincing attachment of a mixer.

Sweet and Sour Sauce

1 small onion
3 canned pineapple rings
40g/1½oz sugar
15g/½oz cornflour
30ml/2 tablespoons vinegar
10ml/2 teaspoons soy sauce
10ml/2 teaspoons
    concentrated tomato purée
a pinch of salt
300ml/½ pint water

Skin the onion. Cut the pineapple into pieces and add to the onion. Chop finely in a blender and keep on one side. Mix the sugar, cornflour, vinegar, soy sauce, tomato purée, salt and water until smooth in a blender. Pour into a pan and simmer gently over low heat, stirring until the sauce thickens. Add the onion and pineapple, and continue simmering for 3 minutes. Serve with pork or chicken.

Make as above, but chop the onion and pineapple finely with the metal blade. Mix the sugar, cornflour, vinegar, soy sauce, tomato purée, salt and water until smooth with the plastic blade.

Tomato Sauce

1 onion
1 garlic clove
15ml/1 tablespoon oil
25g/1oz plain flour
450g/1lb canned tomatoes
5ml/1 teaspoon salt
5ml/1 teaspoon sugar
15ml/1 tablespoon vinegar
15ml/1 tablespoon
    concentrated tomato purée
a pinch of dried mixed herbs
1 bay leaf
a pinch of pepper

Skin the onion and garlic and chop finely (metal blade). Heat the oil in a pan and cook the onion and garlic until soft and golden. Work in the flour and cook for 1 minute. Put into the processor bowl. Sieve the tomatoes and their juice and add to the bowl with the salt, sugar, vinegar, tomato purée and herbs. Mix until smooth (plastic blade). Put into a pan with the bay leaf and pepper. Stir over low heat for 10 minutes. Remove the bay leaf and season to taste.

Make as above, but chop the onion and garlic finely in a blender. Blend the cooked onion mixture, sieved tomatoes, salt, sugar, vinegar, tomato purée, mixed herbs and pepper until smooth before heating.

Vinaigrette Sauce

60ml/4 tablespoons oil
30ml/2 tablespoons wine
   vinegar
2·5ml/½ teaspoon salt
2·5ml/½ teaspoon caster sugar
2·5ml/½ teaspoon mustard
   powder
a pinch of pepper

Process all the ingredients in a blender until smooth. Use for green salads, tomatoes, cold leeks, asparagus, globe artichokes and avocados.

Make as above, but use the plastic blade.

Wine and Mushroom Sauce

1 onion
15g/½oz butter
175g/6oz button mushrooms
300ml/½ pint stock
150ml/¼ pint red wine
15ml/1 tablespoon
   Worcestershire sauce
15g/½oz cornflour
15ml/1 tablespoon water
salt and pepper

Skin the onion and chop it finely (metal blade). Melt the butter and cook the onion until soft and golden. Wipe the mushrooms and chop finely (metal blade). Add to the onion and stir over low heat for 2 minutes. Add the stock, wine and Worcestershire sauce, stir well and simmer for 10 minutes. Cool slightly and return to the processor bowl. Mix the cornflour with the water and add to the bowl. Add salt and pepper. Mix until smooth (plastic blade). Return to the pan and simmer for 5 minutes. Serve with steak or roast beef.

Make as above, but chop the onion finely in a blender. Chop the mushrooms finely in a blender. Blend all the ingredients until smooth before final simmering.

Yoghurt Salad Dressing

150ml/¼ pint natural yoghurt
5ml/1 teaspoon parsley
5ml/1 teaspoon chives
1 thin slice onion
5ml/1 teaspoon made
   mustard

Put the yoghurt, herbs, onion and mustard into the blender, and blend until the herbs are finely chopped. Serve cold with salads or fish. A thick slice of cucumber can be added, if liked (including the skin).

Make as above, using the metal blade to chop the ingredients.

Puddings, Ices and Sweet Sauces

Apple Batter Pudding

450g/1lb eating apples
60ml/4 tablespoons brandy or
    Calvados
a pinch of ground cinnamon
25g/1oz butter
50g/2oz light soft brown
    sugar
3 eggs
150g/5oz self-raising flour
60ml/4 tablespoons milk

Peel and core the apples. Chop them coarsely (metal blade). Put into a bowl with the brandy or Calvados and cinnamon and leave to stand for 1 hour. Use a little of the butter to grease an ovenproof dish. Put in the apples and brandy and sprinkle with the sugar. Dot with flakes of butter. Mix the eggs, flour and milk to a thick cream (plastic blade). Pour over the fruit and bake at 200°C/400°F/Gas Mark 6 for 35 minutes until the batter is crisp and golden. Serve very hot with cream.

Make as above, but chop the apples in a blender. Mix the eggs, flour and milk to a thick cream in a blender.

Apple Meringue

450g/1lb cooking apples
a thin strip of lemon peel
50g/2oz sugar
25g/1oz melted butter
2 egg yolks

Meringue
2 egg whites
100g/4oz caster sugar

Use cooking apples which become fluffy when cooked. Peel and core the apples and cut them into pieces. Put into a saucepan, just cover with water, the lemon peel and sugar, and simmer until the fruit is soft. Cool and put into the blender with the butter and egg yolks and blend until smooth. Put into a pie dish. Whisk the egg whites until stiff with the mixer. Add half the sugar and continue whisking until stiff and glossy. Fold in the remaining sugar by hand, reserving about 1 teaspoon sugar. Spread the meringue mixture on to the apples and sprinkle with the reserved sugar. Bake at 150°C/300°F/Gas Mark 2 for 30 minutes. Serve cold. If liked, the fruit purée may be put into a baked flan case before the meringue is put on top.

Make as above, but chop the apples coarsely, using the metal blade. Blend the cooked fruit with the butter and egg yolks, with the plastic blade.

Apple Popovers

15g/½oz cooking fat
2 medium cooking apples
1oz/25g caster sugar
1 recipe quantity Yorkshire
   Pudding (page 71)
1 lemon
25g/1oz soft brown sugar

Divide the fat between six 10cm/4in patty tins and heat at 220°C/425°F/Gas Mark 7 until the fat is very hot. Peel the apples, core and cut in slices. Toss the apples in caster sugar and divide between the tins. Make up the Yorkshire Pudding batter and add the grated rind of the lemon. Pour over the apples and bake for 30 minutes. Just before serving, put the juice of the lemon and the brown sugar into a saucepan, bring to the boil and boil for 2 minutes until syrupy. Serve spooned into the centres of the popovers.

Make as above, but cut the apples with the slicing disc. Prepare the batter with the plastic blade.

Apple Snow

675g/1½lb cooking apples
5ml/1 teaspoon grated lemon
   rind
5ml/1 teaspoon lemon juice
30ml/2 tablespoons water
50g/2oz caster sugar
2 egg whites
150ml/¼ pint double cream

Use cooking apples which become fluffy when cooked. Peel and slice them, removing the cores. Put into a saucepan with the lemon rind, juice and water. Cook until the apples are soft. Put into the blender with the sugar, and blend until smooth. Cool. Whisk the egg whites with the mixer until stiff peaks form. Turn the mixer to low speed and add the apple in small quantities until it is well mixed in. Put into a bowl. Whip the cream lightly with the mixer, and fold into the apple mixture by hand. Chill before serving. If liked, this mixture may be frozen as ice cream, beaten once during freezing.

Make as above, but slice the apples with the slicing disc or chop them with the metal blade. Process the cooked apples with sugar until smooth, using the plastic blade.

Apricot Crumble

450g/1lb canned apricots
15g/½oz butter
50g/2oz light soft brown
    sugar
a pinch of ground cinnamon

Topping
50g/2oz butter
25g/1oz light soft brown
    sugar
75g/3oz plain flour
a pinch of ground ginger

Drain the apricots and reserve the juice. Chop the fruit coarsely (metal blade). Thoroughly grease an ovenproof dish and put the fruit in it. Dot with flakes of butter and sprinkle with sugar and cinnamon. Add 3 tablespoons syrup from the can. To make the topping, mix the butter, sugar, flour and ginger until the mixture is like coarse breadcrumbs (plastic blade). Sprinkle on top of the fruit and press down very lightly with a fork. Bake at 180°C/350°F/Gas Mark 4 for 45 minutes. Serve hot with cream or custard.

Make as above, but chop the apricots coarsely in a blender. Prepare the crumble mixture in a blender or with a mixer.

Apricot Pudding and Apricot Sauce

450g/1lb canned apricots
175g/6oz stale sponge cake
150ml/¼ pint creamy milk
50g/2oz soft margarine
50g/2oz caster sugar
2 eggs, separated
finely grated rind of 1 orange
2-3 drops almond essence
45ml/3 tablespoons dark
    chunky marmalade

Drain the apricots and reserve the syrup. Chop 8 apricot halves coarsely (metal blade) and keep on one side. Make crumbs with the sponge cake (metal blade) and put them into a bowl with the milk. Leave to stand for 10 minutes. Cream the margarine, sugar and egg yolks with the orange rind and essence (plastic blade). Add the soaked crumbs and chopped apricots and mix just long enough for them to be incorporated. Transfer to another bowl. Whisk the egg whites to soft peaks and fold into the mixture. Grease a pudding basin and put the mixture in it. Cover the basin with a piece of greased greaseproof paper. Cover again with a piece of foil. Put into a saucepan with boiling water to come half-way up the sides of the basin. Cover the pan with a lid and boil for 2 hours, adding more boiling water from time to time so that the pan does not become dry. Turn on to a serving dish.

    Make the sauce by blending the remaining apricots, juice and the marmalade until smooth. Heat through just before serving with the pudding.

Make as above, but chop the apricots coarsely in a blender. Make sponge cake crumbs in a blender. Cream the fat, sugar and yolks with the rind and essence, using a mixer, and gradually add the soaked crumbs and chopped fruit.

    To make the sauce, blend the remaining apricots, juice and marmalade until smooth.

Baked Orange Pudding (page 88)

Baked Orange Pudding

225g/8oz day-old white bread
4 oranges
75g/3oz light soft brown
    sugar
2 eggs and 2 egg yolks
60ml/4 tablespoons brandy

Discard the crusts and make the bread into crumbs (metal blade). Keep on one side. Grate the rind from 2 oranges and mix with the breadcrumbs. Squeeze out all the orange juice. Mix the breadcrumbs, orange juice, sugar, eggs, egg yolks and brandy until well blended (plastic blade). Put the mixture into a greased ovenproof dish. Bake at 180°C/350°F/ Gas Mark 4 for 45 minutes. Serve hot with cream.

Make as above, but prepare the breadcrumbs in a blender. Mix with the orange juice, sugar, eggs, egg yolks and brandy in a blender.

Bakewell Pudding

175g/6oz prepared shortcrust
    pastry (page 122)
50g/2oz strawberry jam
4 eggs
4 drops almond essence
100g/4oz caster sugar
75g/3oz blanched almonds
100g/4oz softened butter
1 thin strip lemon peel

Line a 18cm/7in pie plate with the pastry. Spread the jam on the bottom of the pastry case. Put all the other ingredients into the blender and blend for 30 seconds until well mixed. Pour into the pastry case. Bake at 220°C/425°F/Gas Mark 7 for 25 minutes.

Make as above, but prepare the filling with the plastic blade.

Basic Custard Ice Cream

450ml/¾ pint milk
1 vanilla pod
2 egg yolks
50g/2oz caster sugar
a pinch of salt
150ml/¼ pint double cream

Put the milk into a pan with the vanilla pod. Heat gently until the milk comes to boiling point. Take out the vanilla pod. Cool the milk slightly and then thoroughly blend with the egg yolks, sugar and salt (plastic blade). Pour into the top of a double saucepan or into a bowl over hot water, and heat, stirring constantly, until the mixture is of a coating consistency. Leave to cool. Whip the cream to soft peaks and fold into the custard. Pour into a freezer tray and freeze in the ice-making compartment of the refrigerator at lowest setting for 1 hour. Scoop out the half-frozen mixture into the processor, and mix until smooth (metal blade). Return to the freezer tray and freeze for 1 hour. Scoop out again and mix in the processor until smooth. Return to the freezer tray and freeze for 1 hour. This makes a basic vanilla ice cream.

Make as above, but mix the milk, egg yolks, sugar and salt in the blender. When the mixture is half-frozen, scoop out of the freezer tray and mix until smooth in a blender, or with a mixer.

When making flavoured ice cream, chop the chocolate, nuts, fruit or other additions in a blender before preparing the basic ice cream mixture.

Chocolate Ice Cream
Melt 50g/2oz plain chocolate in 60ml/4 tablespoons hot water and add to the vanilla-flavoured milk before mixing with the egg yolks.

Coffee Ice Cream
Omit the vanilla. Add 15ml/1 tablespoon instant coffee powder to the milk as it is heated before mixing with the eggs.

Tutti Frutti Ice Cream
Add 75g/3oz mixed dried fruit, 25g/1oz chopped mixed candied peel and 25g/1oz chopped nuts to the vanilla ice before freezing.

Blackcurrant Castles

100g/4oz self-raising flour
100g/4oz caster sugar
100g/4oz soft margarine
2 eggs
1·25ml/¼ teaspoon vanilla
essence
30ml/2 tablespoons warm
water
20ml/4 teaspoons
blackcurrant jam

Put the flour, sugar, margarine, eggs and essence into the mixer bowl and mix to a soft consistency. Add the water and mix until well blended in. Place 4 greased castle pudding tins on a baking sheet and put a spoonful of jam in the base of each tin. Cover with the sponge mixture. Bake at 180°C/350°F/Gas Mark 4 for 25 minutes. Turn out and serve hot with some additional hot blackcurrant jam.

Make as above, but mix the margarine, sugar, eggs, flour and essence with the plastic blade. Add the water through the feeder tube with the motor running.

Brown Bread Ice Cream and Apricot Sauce

100g/4oz day-old brown
bread
300ml/½ pint double cream
150ml/¼ pint single cream
75g/3oz icing sugar
15ml/1 tablespoon rum
2 eggs, separated

Apricot Sauce
450g/1lb canned apricots
60ml/4 tablespoons dark
chunky marmalade

Discard the crusts and cut the bread into pieces. Make into crumbs (metal blade). Spread the crumbs on a baking sheet, and bake at 150°C/300°F/Gas Mark 2 for 10 minutes. Leave until cold. Whip the double cream until just stiff and gradually pour in the single cream whipping to soft peaks. Put into the processor. Add the icing sugar, rum and egg yolks, and mix for 10 seconds (plastic blade). Add the crumbs and mix for 5 seconds. Whisk the egg whites to soft peaks and fold into the mixture. Pour into an ice tray and freeze in the ice compartment of the refrigerator at lowest setting for 3 hours. This ice cream does not need beating while freezing.

Prepare the sauce by blending the apricots, syrup and marmalade until smooth (metal blade). Chill the sauce while the ice cream is freezing. Spoon the ice cream into glasses and serve with sauce.

Make as above, but prepare the breadcrumbs in a blender. Whip the cream with the whisk attachment of a mixer. Mix with the icing sugar, rum, yolks and crumbs in a blender. Whisk the egg whites with the whisk attachment. Prepare the sauce in a blender.

Right Brown Bread Ice Cream and Apricot Sauce

Chocolate Almond Pudding

24 sponge fingers (boudoir
  biscuits)
100g/4oz plain chocolate
100g/4oz butter
50g/2oz caster sugar
100g/4oz ground almonds
150ml/¼ pint double cream
50ml/2fl oz milk

Dip the sponge fingers into milk for a second so they are just moist, and arrange in a neat circle in a cake tin with removable base. Melt the chocolate and pour into the mixer basin. Add the butter, sugar and almonds, and beat until smooth and creamy. Whip the cream to soft peaks and fold into the chocolate mixture together with any remaining milk. Pour into the tin and leave for 12 hours in the refrigerator. Turn out and decorate with more whipped cream if liked, or some grated chocolate.

Make as above, but prepare the butter, sugar and almonds with the metal or plastic blade. Add whipped cream and any remaining milk and process only just until the mixture is well blended.

Chocolate Bread Pudding

175g/6oz day-old white bread
100g/4oz plain chocolate
150ml/¼ pint milk
75g/3oz butter
100g/4oz caster sugar
2 eggs, separated
1·25ml/¼ teaspoon vanilla
  essence

Discard the crusts and make bread into crumbs (metal blade). Keep on one side. Grate the chocolate (grating disc). Put the milk and butter into a pan and bring to the boil. Take off the heat and stir in the grated chocolate until melted. Add the breadcrumbs and simmer for 10 minutes. Cool this mixture and return to the processor bowl. Add the sugar, egg yolks and essence. Mix until well blended (plastic blade), then transfer to another bowl. Whisk the egg whites to stiff peaks and fold into the chocolate mixture. Thoroughly grease a pudding basin and put the mixture in it. Cover the basin with a piece of greased greaseproof paper. Cover again with a piece of foil. Put into a saucepan with boiling water to come half-way up the sides of the basin. Cover the pan with a lid and boil for 2 hours, adding more boiling water from time to time so that the pan does not become dry. Turn out and serve hot with cream or chocolate sauce.

Make as above, but prepare the breadcrumbs in a blender. Chop the chocolate finely in a blender, warm the milk and butter and blend until the chocolate has dissolved. Simmer this mixture with the breadcrumbs for 10 minutes, cool and then blend with the sugar, egg yolks and essence.

Chocolate Brownies

225g/8oz granulated sugar
40g/1½oz cocoa powder
75g/3oz self-raising flour
a pinch of salt
2 eggs
30ml/2 tablespoons creamy milk
100g/4oz melted butter or
   margarine
50g/2oz shelled nuts
100g/4oz plain chocolate
25g/1oz butter

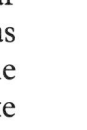

Stir together the sugar, cocoa powder, flour and salt in the mixer bowl. Add the eggs, milk and melted fat, and mix on low speed until well mixed; do not overbeat. Chop the nuts in the blender and add to the mixture. Pour into a rectangular tin about 20 × 30cm/8 × 12in, and bake at 180°C/350°F/Gas Mark 4 for 30 minutes. Cool in the tin and then pour on the chocolate melted with the butter. Cool until the chocolate has set and cut into squares.

Make as above, but chop the nuts first with the metal blade. Mix the eggs, milk, fat and nuts with the plastic blade.

Chocolate Chiffon Pie

150g/5oz plain chocolate
   digestive biscuits
100g/4oz butter
100g/4oz sugar

Filling
300ml/½ pint whipping cream
10ml/2 teaspoons gelatine
30ml/2 tablespoons water
250ml/8fl oz milk
50g/2oz plain chocolate
3 eggs, separated
100g/4oz sugar
a pinch of salt
3 drops vanilla essence

Crush the biscuits into crumbs (metal blade). Melt the butter in a pan and add the sugar and crumbs. Press into the base of a 25cm/10in ovenproof dish and bake at 180°C/350°F/Gas Mark 4 for 15 minutes. Cool at room temperature and then chill in the refrigerator until firm.

To make the filling, whip the cream to soft peaks and keep on one side. Mix the gelatine and water in a small bowl or cup and put the bowl into a pan of hot water, stirring until the mixture is syrupy. Heat the milk and chocolate together until just below boiling point. Mix the egg yolks (plastic blade). Start the machine, pour in the sugar, salt and essence through the feeder tube, and gradually pour in the milk mixture. When the eggs and milk are combined, return to the saucepan and cook very gently until the mixture thickens like custard. Remove from the heat and cool for 10 minutes, then stir in the gelatine. Leave until thick and cool. Mix with the cream just long enough to blend together (plastic blade), then turn into another bowl. Whisk the egg whites to stiff peaks. Fold into the cream mixture and pour on to the biscuit base. Chill before serving. If liked, decorate with some grated plain chocolate, or with whirls of whipped cream and grated chocolate.

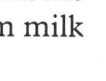

Make as above, but prepare the crumbs in a blender. Mix the egg yolks in a blender and gradually pour in the warm milk mixture through the lid, with the machine running.

Chocolate Chiffon Pie

Chocolate Sauce

100g/4oz plain chocolate
225g/8oz sugar
150ml/¼ pint hot coffee or
    milk
a pinch of salt
2·5ml/½ teaspoon vanilla
    essence

Chop the chocolate finely in the blender. Put all the ingredients into the blender and blend until smooth. Cool and store in a covered jar in the refrigerator.

Make as above, but use the metal blade to chop the chocolate. Blend all the ingredients with the metal blade.

Coffee Cream Flan

225g/8oz prepared shortcrust
    pastry (page 122)
30ml/2 tablespoons apricot
    jam
75g/3oz butter
75g/3oz caster sugar
1 egg
50g/2oz walnuts
225g/8oz self-raising flour
15ml/1 tablespoon coffee
    essence
15ml/1 tablespoon milk
150ml/¼ pint soured cream

Roll out the pastry and use to line a 20cm/8in flan ring. Spread apricot jam on the base. Put the butter into the mixing bowl with caster sugar and mix on low speed until light and fluffy. Work in the egg, walnuts chopped in the blender, flour, coffee essence and milk. When the mixture is smooth and light, put into the pastry case. Bake at 220°C/425°F/Gas Mark 7 for 15 minutes, and then at 160°C/325°F/Gas Mark 3 for 30 minutes. Spread the soured cream on top and bake for 2 minutes. Serve hot.

Make as above, but cream the butter and caster sugar (plastic blade). Add the egg, chopped nuts, flour, essence and milk and process until smooth and light. Walnuts can be chopped in a blender, or processed with metal blade and kept on one side while the coffee mixture is being prepared.

Coventry Tarts

225g/8oz prepared shortcrust
    pastry (page 122)
225g/8oz cottage cheese
100g/4oz caster sugar
a pinch of salt
a pinch of ground nutmeg
15ml/1 tablespoon orange
    juice
50g/2oz melted butter
1 egg
60ml/4 tablespoons apple,
    redcurrant or cranberry
    jelly

Roll out the pastry to line 16 tartlet tins. Put the cottage cheese, sugar, salt, nutmeg, orange juice, cool melted butter and egg into the blender and blend on low speed until smooth and creamy. Fill the pastry cases two-thirds full with the mixture. Bake at 190°C/375°F/Gas Mark 5 for 20 minutes until the pastry is golden and the filling is set and lightly coloured. Serve freshly baked with a spoonful of jelly on each one.

Make as above, but blend the filling ingredients with the plastic blade.

Custard Sauce

1 egg
50g/2oz caster sugar
25g/1oz butter
2·5ml/½ teaspoon vanilla
  essence
600ml/1 pint milk
25g/1oz cornflour

Mix the egg, sugar, butter and essence until creamy (plastic blade). Mix 45ml/3 tablespoons milk with the cornflour. Heat the rest of the milk to boiling point. Pour on to the cornflour and return to the pan. Cook for 2 minutes over low heat, stirring all the time. With the machine running, pour the milk mixture slowly through the feeder tube and continue processing until smooth. Serve hot or cold.

Make as above, but mix the egg, sugar, butter and essence in a blender. Pour the hot cornflour and milk mixture through the lid with the machine running.

Eve's Pudding

450g/1lb cooking apples
75g/3oz light soft brown
  sugar
100g/4oz soft margarine
100g/4oz caster sugar
100g/4oz self-raising flour
2 eggs
grated rind of 1 lemon
1·25ml/¼ teaspoon vanilla
  essence
extra caster sugar

Peel and core the apples. Cut them into pieces and chop coarsely (metal blade). Grease an ovenproof dish and put the apples in it. Sprinkle with the brown sugar. Mix the fruit and sugar lightly together. Put the margarine, caster sugar, flour, eggs, lemon rind and essence into the processor bowl and mix to a soft dough (plastic blade). Spread over the apples. Bake at 180°C/350°F/Gas Mark 4 for 40 minutes. Sprinkle with caster sugar and serve at once with cream or custard.

Prepare as above, but use a blender to chop the apples. Prepare the sponge mixture with a mixer.

Fresh Fruit Fool

225g/8oz fresh raspberries,
  strawberries or blackberries
75g/3oz caster sugar
grated rind of ½ orange
5ml/1 teaspoon lemon juice
150ml/¼ pint double cream

Wash and hull the berries. Mix to a purée with the sugar, orange rind and lemon juice (metal blade). Put the purée through a sieve to get rid of any pips. Whip the cream to soft peaks and put into processor. With the machine running, pour in the fruit purée through the feeder tube until the cream and fruit are just mixed. Spoon into tall glasses and chill for an hour before serving. The fool may be decorated with a whirl of whipped cream topped with a piece of fresh fruit.

(CONTINUES)

Make as above, but purée the fruit in a blender, then sieve. If available, prepare the fruit with the colander-and-sieve attachment of a mixer. Mix the fruit purée and cream in a blender or with a mixer.

Frozen Orange Pudding

12 macaroons
1 orange
1 lemon
3 eggs, separated
100g/4oz sugar
a pinch of salt
300ml/½ pint double cream

Break the macaroons into pieces and make into coarse crumbs (metal blade). Sprinkle half the crumbs in an ice-making tray and reserve the rest. Squeeze out the orange and lemon juice. Beat the juices, egg yolks, sugar and salt until well mixed (plastic bowl). Pour into the top of a double saucepan or a bowl over boiling water, and cook until thick and creamy. Leave until cool. Whip the cream to soft peaks. Whisk the egg whites to stiff peaks. Fold the cream and then the egg whites into the orange mixture. Pour on top of the macaroon crumbs. Top with the remaining crumbs. Freeze in the ice-making compartment of a refrigerator at lowest setting for 4 hours. Put into the main part of the refrigerator for 1 hour before serving. Turn on to a serving dish and cut into thick slices.

Make as above, but prepare the crumbs in a blender. Mix the juices, egg yolks, sugar and salt in a blender.

Fruited Fritters

100g/4oz plain flour
a pinch of salt
1 egg
90ml/6 tablespoons milk
15g/½oz icing sugar
grated rind of 1 orange
100g/4oz mixed dried fruit
25g/1oz chopped mixed peel
50g/2oz caster sugar

Put the flour, salt, egg, milk and icing sugar into the blender and mix until smooth and creamy. Add the orange rind, dried fruit and peel. Heat about 2·5cm/1in oil in a frying pan, and fry teaspoonfuls of the mixture in the oil for about 3 minutes, turning once, until golden and crisp. Drain on absorbent paper and toss in caster sugar before serving very hot. A little warmed marmalade may be served with these fritters as a sauce.

Make as above, but prepare the batter with the plastic blade.

Fruit Mousse

350g/12oz fruit
sugar to taste
25g/1oz gelatine
15ml/1 tablespoon lemon
 juice
2 eggs, separated

The fruit may be fresh, canned or frozen. If the fresh or frozen fruit is juicy (eg raspberries), no further liquid will be required. Other fruit should be cooked in a little water until just soft. Sweeten the fruit lightly to taste. Put the gelatine into 30ml/2 tablespoons water, and stand the bowl in hot water until the gelatine melts and is syrupy. Put the fruit into the blender with a little cooking liquid, or syrup from the can. Add the gelatine, lemon juice and egg yolks. Blend for 1 minute. Put into a bowl and leave in a cool place until nearly set. Whisk the egg whites until stiff, and fold into the fruit mixture gently by hand. Leave until set.

Make as above, but blend the fruit mixture with the plastic blade.

Golden Pineapple Sponge

25g/1oz butter
30ml/2 tablespoons dark soft
 brown sugar
450g/1lb canned pineapple
 rings
6 glacé cherries
100g/4oz soft margarine
100g/4oz caster sugar
2 eggs
100g/4oz self-raising flour

Grease a pie dish liberally with butter. Sprinkle with the brown sugar. Drain the pineapple rings and arrange 6 rings in the base of the pie dish. Place a cherry in the centre of each ring. Chop the remaining pineapple coarsely (metal blade) and keep on one side. Mix the margarine and sugar with the eggs and flour until well creamed (plastic blade). Stir in the chopped pineapple and spread over the pineapple rings in the pie dish. Bake at 180°C/350°F/Gas Mark 4 for 45 minutes. Turn out and serve with custard.

Make as above, but chop the pineapple in a blender. Prepare the sponge mixture with a mixer.

Jelly Whip

150ml/¼ pint water
1 × 600ml/1 pint pkt fruit jelly
1 × 170g/6oz can evaporated
 milk

Boil the water in a small saucepan, reduce the heat and put in the jelly, broken into pieces. Simmer until the jelly has melted. Put the evaporated milk in the blender, and blend until light and fluffy. With the blender running, slowly pour in the liquid jelly and continue blending until well mixed. Pour into a bowl and chill. If liked, blend a little fruit

(CONTINUES)

with the jelly, such as raspberries with raspberry jelly, or pineapple with pineapple jelly.

Make as above, but mix the jelly mixture until well blended, using the plastic blade.

Lemon Cheesecake

50g/2oz digestive biscuits
450g/1lb cottage cheese
5ml/1 teaspoon lemon juice
5ml/1 teaspoon grated lemon rind
5ml/1 teaspoon grated orange rind
15ml/1 tablespoon cornflour
2 eggs, separated
30ml/2 tablespoons double cream
100g/4oz caster sugar

Break up the biscuits and make into crumbs (metal blade). Grease a 20cm/8in round cake tin with removable base and line the base with greased greaseproof paper. Sprinkle the crumbs on the base. Mix the cottage cheese, lemon juice and rind, orange rind, cornflour, egg yolks and cream until smooth (plastic blade). Transfer to another bowl. Whisk the egg whites to stiff peaks. Add half the sugar and whisk until stiff. Fold in the remaining sugar with a metal spoon. Fold this meringue mixture into the cheese mixture. Pour on top of the biscuits. Bake at 180°C/350°F/Gas Mark 4 for 1 hour. Turn off the oven and leave the cheesecake until cold. Remove from the tin and serve with fresh, canned or frozen fruit.

Make as above, but prepare the crumbs in a blender. Prepare the cheese mixture in a blender and transfer to a bowl before the meringue mixture is folded in.

Lemon Flummery

300ml/½ pint water
25g/1oz butter
rind and juice of 1 lemon
25g/1oz plain flour
100g/4oz caster sugar
1 size 1-2 egg, separated
4 digestive biscuits

Put the water into a pan with the butter and grated lemon rind, and bring to the boil. Remove from the heat and cool slightly. Put the juice of the lemon, flour and sugar into the blender, and pour on the liquid. Blend for 30 seconds. Add the egg yolk and blend for 5 seconds. Put the mixture into a saucepan and bring slowly to the boil, stirring gently. Simmer for 10 minutes and pour into a bowl. Whisk the egg white until stiff, and fold into the lemon mixture. Chill until cold and firm. Break up the biscuits and blend to coarse crumbs. Sprinkle on top of the flummery, and serve with cream.

Make as above, but prepare the lemon mixture with the plastic blade. Prepare the crumbs with the metal blade.

Lemon Mousse

150ml/¼ pint water
3 lemons
225g/8oz sugar
4 eggs, separated
15g/½oz gelatine
300ml/½ pint double cream

Put the water into a pan. Grate the rind of 1 lemon and squeeze the juice from all three. Add to the pan with the sugar. Bring to the boil, stirring well, and boil for 5 minutes. Mix the egg yolks until well blended (plastic blade). With the machine running, pour the hot syrup through the feeder tube on to the egg yolks and process until the mixture is light and fluffy. Put the gelatine into a cup with 4 tablespoons water and stand in a pan of hot water. Heat until the gelatine is syrupy. Add to the egg mixture and process just enough to mix. Pour into a bowl and cool until the mixture is just beginning to set. Whip the cream to soft peaks. Whisk the egg whites to stiff peaks. Fold the cream and then the egg whites into the lemon mixture. Pour into a serving bowl and chill.

Make as above, but mix the lemon syrup and egg yolks in a blender, and add the gelatine mixture through the lid with the machine running.

Lilian's Lemon Flan

100g/4oz butter
225g/8oz gingernut biscuits
juice of 2 lemons
1 × 196g/6·9oz can condensed milk
150ml/¼ pint double cream

Melt the butter until just soft. Break the biscuits in pieces and make into crumbs in the blender. Mix with the butter and press into a lightly greased flan case. Put the lemon juice, condensed milk and cream in the mixer bowl, and whip to soft peaks. Pour into the flan case and chill before serving.

Make as above, but prepare the crumbs with the metal blade. Combine the lemon juice, condensed milk and cream with the plastic blade, processing until thick and creamy.

Queen of Puddings

6 × 2·5cm/1in thick slices
  bread
450ml/¾ pint milk
50g/2oz sugar
1 thin strip lemon peel
50g/2oz butter
2 eggs, separated
25g/1oz strawberry jam
25g/1oz caster sugar

Tear the bread into small pieces and blend into crumbs. Put into a bowl. Warm the milk without boiling, and put into the blender with the sugar, lemon peel, butter and egg yolks, and blend for 10 seconds. Pour over the crumbs, stir well, and put into a greased pie dish. Bake at 160°C/325°F/ Gas Mark 3 for 30 minutes. Spread the jam on top of the pudding. Whisk the egg whites until they form soft peaks. Gradually beat in the caster sugar until the mixture is stiff and glossy. Spread on top of the jam, and continue baking for 15 minutes.

Make as above, but prepare the crumbs with the metal blade. Add the warm milk, sugar, lemon peel, butter and egg yolks, and process until well mixed.

Raspberry Sauce

225g/8oz raspberries
50g/2oz icing sugar

Blend the fruit and sugar to a thick purée, adding a little water if too thick. Put through a sieve and chill. If a colander-and-sieve attachment to the mixer is available, this may be used instead of blending and sieving.

Make as above, but use the metal or plastic blade to blend the fruit and sugar. Sieve to remove pips.

Raspberry Water Ice

100g/4oz sugar
300ml/½ pint water
450g/1lb raspberries

Put the sugar and water in a saucepan, bring to the boil, boil for 5 minutes, and then cool. Blend the raspberries and sieve them (or use a colander-and-sieve attachment on the mixer). Put the raspberry purée and sugar syrup into the blender, and blend for 15 seconds. Pour into a freezer tray and freeze for 3 hours. Half-way through freezing, blend the mixture again. For a lighter ice, fold in a stiffly whisked egg white at this stage. The same method can be used for blackberries, strawberries or blackcurrants, but blackcurrants need to be cooked in a little water before blending.

(CONTINUES)

Make as in the main method on page 101, but use the plastic or metal blade to process the raspberries. Sieve them and return to the clean processor bowl with the sugar syrup. Process until well mixed before freezing. Half-way through freezing, process until smooth, using the metal blade.

Rhubarb Toffee Pudding

25g/1oz butter
50g/2oz light soft brown
   sugar
675g/1½lb rhubarb
225g/8oz self-raising flour
1 teaspoon salt
75g/3oz shredded suet
150ml/¼ pint cold water
½ lemon
100g/4oz sugar
50g/2oz sultanas
25g/1oz chopped mixed
   candied peel
a pinch of ground cinnamon
90ml/6 tablespoons water

Grease a pudding basin liberally with the butter and sprinkle with the brown sugar. Wash and trim the rhubarb, cut in pieces and chop coarsely (metal blade). Keep the rhubarb on one side. Mix the flour, salt, suet and cold water to a soft dough (plastic blade). Cut off one-third for a lid. Roll out the remaining dough very lightly and line the pudding basin. Put in half the rhubarb. Grate the rind of the lemon and squeeze out the juice. In a bowl, mix the sugar, sultanas, peel, grated rind and juice of the lemon, and the cinnamon. Sprinkle this mixture on to the rhubarb and cover with the remaining rhubarb. Add the water. Cover with the remaining dough. Grease a piece of greaseproof paper and place on top. Bake at 180°C/350°F/Gas Mark 4 for 1¼ hours. Turn out and serve with cream or custard.

Make as above, but chop the rhubarb coarsely in a blender. Make the dough with a mixer.

Rum Butter

225g/8oz unsalted butter
225g/8oz light soft brown
   sugar
90ml/6 tablespoons light rum

Cut the butter into small pieces and process until soft (plastic blade). Add half the sugar and process until light and fluffy. With the machine running, add the remaining sugar and the rum in small amounts through the feeder tube until well mixed. This must be done slowly or the mixture may curdle. Put into a serving dish and chill. Serve with puddings or mince pies, or as a spread on biscuits.

Make as above, but use a mixer on slow speed.

Left Queen of Puddings (page 101)

Sweet Soufflés

50g/2oz plain flour
300ml/½ pint milk
3 size 1-2 eggs, separated
75g/3oz butter
50g/2oz caster sugar

Put the flour, milk and egg yolks into the blender and blend on low speed until smooth. Melt the butter and stir in the milk mixture and sugar, cooking gently and stirring well until smooth and thick. Remove from the heat. Whisk the egg whites to stiff peaks and fold into the sauce. Grease a 1·2 litre/2 pint soufflé dish, fill with the mixture and bake at 190°C/375°F/Gas Mark 5 for 45 minutes. Serve and eat at once. This method of cooking gives a crisp crust. For a softer soufflé, bake the dish in a pan of hot but not boiling water in the oven.

Make as above, but prepare the flour, milk and egg yolks with the plastic blade.

Flavourings

Apple
Add 60ml/4 tablespoons sweet cooked apples and a squeeze of lemon juice to the cooked sauce, blend for 10 seconds, and fold in egg whites.

Apricot
Add 6 canned apricot halves to the cooked sauce and blend for 10 seconds before folding in egg whites.

Chocolate
Blend 50g/2oz plain chocolate with the milk mixture before cooking the sauce.

Lemon
Add the grated rind and juice of 1 lemon to the sauce before folding in the egg whites.

Liqueur
Stir in 75ml/5 tablespoons Cointreau or Grand Marnier just before folding in the egg whites.

Soft Fruit
Add 150ml/¼ pint sieved raspberries or strawberries to the cooked sauce and blend for 10 seconds before folding in the egg whites.

Breads, Pastry, Cakes, Biscuits and Icings

Almond Paste

225g/8oz ground almonds
100g/4oz icing sugar
100g/4oz caster sugar
5ml/1 teaspoon lemon juice
5ml/1 teaspoon almond
   essence
1 egg

Mix the almonds, icing sugar, caster sugar, lemon juice and essence just long enough for them to be well blended (plastic blade). In a bowl beat the egg lightly with a fork. With the machine running, add the egg through the feeder tube until the mixture blends into a firm paste. Do not overwork the paste or the oil will run out and discolour any icing placed on top. Two eggs may be necessary if they are small. Egg yolks may be used for almond paste (and the whites used for a royal icing) but this gives a dark yellow paste. For a pale and delicate almond paste, use egg whites only.

Make as above, but mixing the dry ingredients with a mixer and gradually add the lemon juice, almond essence and egg until a firm paste is formed. Be careful not to overwork the paste.

Banana Bread

3 ripe bananas
225g/8oz plain flour
3 teaspoons baking powder
a pinch of salt
50g/2oz soft margarine
50g/2oz light soft brown
   sugar
grated rind of 1 lemon
1 egg
45-60ml/3-4 tablespoons milk

Cut the bananas into pieces. Chop them in a blender until they are puréed, then put on one side. Add all the other ingredients gradually through the hole in the lid with the machine running, until a soft batter is formed. If necessary, add a little more milk. Put the mixture into a 450g/1lb greased and floured loaf tin, and bake at 190°C/375°F/Gas Mark 5 for 45 minutes. Turn out and cool on a wire rack. Serve sliced and buttered.

Make as above, but purée the bananas with the metal blade. Mix the flour, baking powder, salt, margarine, sugar and lemon rind until well blended, using the plastic blade. Gradually pour in the mixed egg and milk through the feeder tube to make a soft batter.

Scones, sandwich cake, fruit buns, gingerbread and other tea-time favourites

Basic Sandwich Cake

175g/6oz self-raising flour
7·5ml/1½ teaspoons baking
   powder
175g/6oz soft margarine
175g/6oz caster sugar
3 eggs

Sift the flour and baking powder into the processor bowl. Add the remaining ingredients and process until light and fluffy (plastic blade). Grease two 18cm/7in sandwich tins and divide the mixture between them. Bake at 180°C/350°F/Gas Mark 4 for 30 minutes. Cool on a wire rack.

Make as above but use a mixer; omit the baking powder. Put all the ingredients into the mixing bowl and cream until light and fluffy.

Chocolate Sandwich

Add 25g/1oz cocoa and 15ml/1 tablespoon milk to ingredients. Finish with chocolate butter cream for the filling and topping, and sprinkle with 50g/2oz chopped walnuts.

Coffee Sandwich

Add 15ml/1 tablespoon coffee essence to ingredients. Finish with coffee butter cream for filling and topping.

Cream Sandwich

Whip 150ml/$\frac{1}{4}$ pint double cream to soft peaks. Spread a little jam on one cake, top with cream and put on the second cake. Sprinkle the top with caster or icing sugar. Chopped fresh, canned or frozen fruit may be mixed with the cream.

Jam Sandwich

Sandwich the cakes together with jam and sprinkle the top with caster sugar or sieved icing sugar.

Lemon or Orange Sandwich

Add 1 teaspoon grated lemon or orange rind and 1 tablespoon lemon or orange juice to the ingredients. Finish with the appropriate cream for filling and topping.

Basic White Bread

7g/$\frac{1}{4}$oz fresh yeast
150ml/$\frac{1}{4}$ pint warm water
225g/8oz strong plain flour
5ml/1 teaspoon salt
15g/$\frac{1}{2}$oz lard
poppy, caraway or sesame
 seeds, optional

Blend the fresh yeast in the warm water. Mix the flour, salt and lard (plastic blade). Add the yeast liquid and mix for 1 minute. Yeast may also be added through the feeder tube, with the machine running. Flour your hands lightly and shape the dough into a ball. Oil a polythene bag and put the dough in it. Leave in a warm place for about 1 hour until the dough has doubled in size. Return the dough to the mixer bowl and mix for 1 minute (plastic blade). Shape the dough into the required shape and return to the oiled polythene bag. Leave to prove for 40 minutes. Remove from the bag. Sprinkle with poppy, caraway or sesame seeds, if you wish, and bake at 220°C/425°F/Gas Mark 7 for 30 minutes. Cool on a wire rack.

Make as above, but knead the dough with the dough hook of a mixer.

Brown Bread

Substitute wholemeal flour for half the white flour.

Butter Icing (mixer)

75g/3oz butter
175g/6oz icing sugar
flavouring

Warm the bowl and mixer beater. Put the butter, sugar and flavouring into the bowl and mix on low speed until light and fluffy.

Butter Icing (blender)

30ml/2 tablespoons liquid
75g/3oz butter
175g/6oz icing sugar
flavouring

The liquid may be fruit juice, thin cream or strong coffee. The butter should be soft but not melted. Put all the ingredients into the blender and blend until smooth and light.

Butter Icing (processor)

175g/6oz butter
350g/12oz icing sugar
flavouring

The butter should be soft but not melted. Sift the icing sugar and mix with the butter and flavouring until light and fluffy (plastic blade).

Flavourings

Chocolate
Add 15g/½oz cocoa or 50g/2oz melted plain chocolate.

Coffee
Add 10ml/2 teaspoons coffee essence.

Lemon
Add 5ml/1 teaspoon lemon juice and 1 teaspoon grated lemon rind (or a few drops of lemon essence).

Mocha
Add 15g/½oz cocoa and a few drops of coffee essence.

Orange
Add 10ml/2 teaspoons orange juice and 1 teaspoon grated orange rind (or a few drops of orange essence).

Vanilla
Add a few drops of vanilla essence.

Cheese Pastry

175g/6oz plain flour
a pinch of salt
a pinch of Cayenne pepper
50g/2oz butter
50g/2oz cheese
30ml/2 tablespoons cold water

Put the flour, salt, Cayenne pepper and cut-up butter into the mixing bowl, switch to minimum speed, and rub into fine crumbs, increasing the speed as the fat breaks up. Shred the cheese with a shredder attachment and add to the mixture, and then add the water. Switch off as soon as the liquid is mixed in. Roll out to use for savoury pies and flans.

Make as above, but grate the cheese first with the grating disc. Prepare the pastry with the plastic blade.

Chocolate Chip Orange Cakes

1 orange
50g/2oz plain chocolate
50g/2oz soft margarine
50g/2oz caster sugar
1 egg
75g/3oz self-raising flour

Grate the rind from the orange and squeeze out the juice. Chop the chocolate finely (metal blade). Mix the margarine, sugar, egg and flour with the orange rind and juice until light and soft (plastic blade). Stir in the chocolate pieces. Put into 12 paper cases on a baking sheet. Bake at 190°C/375°F/Gas Mark 5 for 15 minutes. Cool on a wire rack.

Make as above, but chop the chocolate finely in a blender. Cream the margarine, sugar, egg, flour, orange rind and juice with a mixer until light and soft.

Choux Pastry

100g/4oz butter
300ml/½ pint water
150g/5oz plain flour
a pinch of salt
4 eggs

Put the butter and water into a pan and bring to the boil. Tip in all the flour and salt at once and cook gently, stirring well for 2 minutes until the mixture leaves the sides of the pan. Cool for 10 minutes and put into the processor bowl (plastic blade). With the machine running, add the eggs one at a time through the feeder tube, mixing until completely incorporated. Use as required.

Make as above, but use a mixer. Add the eggs one at a time, with the machine running, until the mixture is thick and creamy.

(CONTINUES)

Choux Buns

Lightly grease a baking sheet. Put 15 heaps of the choux pastry mixture (page 109) on to the baking sheet. Bake at 200°C/400°F/Gas Mark 6 for 30 minutes. Lift on to a wire rack and cut a small slit in the bottom of each bun to allow steam to escape. Whip 300ml/½ pint double cream until thick enough to pipe, and pipe into the buns. Sprinkle with sifted icing sugar. Alternatively, spoon on melted chocolate or glacé icing.

Eclairs

Grease baking sheets and pipe the mixture with a plain 1cm/½in nozzle in 10cm/4in lengths. Proceed as for Choux Buns.

Confectioner's Custard

50g/2oz sugar
2 egg yolks
a few drops vanilla essence
300ml/½ pint milk
25g/1oz plain flour
15g/½oz butter

Put the sugar, egg yolks, essence, milk and flour into the blender and blend for 30 seconds until creamy. Put into a thick pan and cook gently, stirring well, until thick. Add the butter and cool. Use for filling cakes, choux pastry, slices, and the bases of fruit flans.

Make as above, but use the plastic blade.

Cornish Splits

450g/1lb strong plain flour
50g/2oz caster sugar
150ml/¼ pint milk
150ml/¼ pint water
25g/1oz fresh yeast
5ml/1 teaspoon salt
50g/2oz butter

Sieve one-quarter of the flour into a bowl and stir in 1 teaspoon sugar. Warm the milk and water together to lukewarm, stir in the yeast and add to the flour. Mix with the mixer on low speed until well blended and leave 30 minutes until frothy. Sift the remaining flour and salt and stir in the remaining sugar. Add to the yeast mixture with the melted and cooled butter, and work with the dough hook to give a light soft dough. Cover and leave until doubled in size. Turn on to a floured board, knead lightly and divide into 14 pieces. Form into round buns and put on buttered and floured baking trays, leaving space to rise. Leave for 30 minutes. Bake at 220°C/425°F/Gas Mark 7 for 20 minutes. Cool on a wire rack, split diagonally and fill with jam and whipped cream.

Make as above, but mix the dough with the plastic blade.

Date and Walnut Cake (page 112)

Crumb Fingers

225g/8oz plain flour
175g/6oz block margarine
100g/4oz sugar
10ml/2 teaspoons grated
    lemon rind
a pinch of ground ginger

Sift the flour into a mixer bowl. Cut the fat into small pieces, and, with the mixer on low speed, work the fat into the flour until it is rubbed in. Add the sugar, lemon rind and ginger, and continue mixing until the mixture is like fine breadcrumbs. Press the mixture into a greased 20cm/8in square tin, and press down very lightly with a fork. Bake at 160°C/325°F/Gas Mark 3 for 30 minutes. Leave in the tin for 10 minutes and mark into fingers with a sharp knife. Leave until completely cold and cut into fingers.

Make as above, but use the plastic blade to rub in the fat and to process it with the sugar, lemon rind and ginger.

Date and Walnut Cake

50g/2oz walnut halves
225g/8oz stoned dates
175g/6oz soft margarine
175g/6oz light soft brown
    sugar
225g/8oz plain flour
7·5ml/1½ teaspoons baking
    powder
3 eggs
30ml/2 tablespoons milk
45ml/3 tablespoons icing
    sugar

Chop the walnuts coarsely (metal blade). Chop the dates finely (metal blade). Keep the dates and walnuts on one side. Cream the margarine and sugar until light and fluffy (plastic blade). Sift together the flour and baking powder. Add the eggs, one at a time, with a little of the flour and milk through the feeder tube, mixing for 10 seconds after each addition. Add the remaining flour and mix just long enough for the flour to be incorporated. Stir in the dates and nuts. Put the mixture in a 900g/2lb greased loaf tin, and bake at 160°C/325°F/Gas Mark 3 for 1½ hours. Cool in the tin for 10 minutes, then turn out on to a wire rack to finish cooling. Sift the icing sugar over the top just before serving.

Make as above, chopping the walnuts coarsely in a blender. Keep on one side. Chop the dates finely in a blender and keep on one side. Prepare the cake mixture with a mixer before folding in the dates and nuts.

225g/8oz eating apples
100g/4oz butter
100g/4oz sugar
1 egg
225g/8oz plain flour
7·5ml/1½ teaspoons baking
    powder
a pinch of salt
blanched almonds

Filling
75g/3oz butter
75g/3oz light soft brown
    sugar

Dorset Apple Cake

Peel and core the apples. Cut them into quarters and then
chop coarsely (metal blade). Keep the apples on one side.
Cream the butter and sugar until light and fluffy (plastic
blade). Add the egg, and cream the mixture for 10 seconds.
Sift together the flour, baking powder and salt. Add to the
creamed mixture and mix for a few seconds until incorporated. Stir in the chopped apple. Grease a 20cm/8in round
cake tin and put the mixture in it. Bake at 180°C/350°F/Gas
Mark 4 for 50 minutes. Turn on to a wire rack to cool. After
10 minutes, split through the cake with a sharp knife.

 To make the filling, cream the butter and brown sugar
until light and fluffy (plastic blade). Spread half the mixture
between the pieces of cake, and use the rest to spread on top.
Decorate with almonds. Eat freshly baked.

Make as above, but chop the apples in a blender. Prepare the
cake mixture with a mixer before stirring in the chopped
apple. Prepare the filling by creaming the butter and sugar
with a mixer.

Drop Scones

225g/8oz plain flour
a pinch of salt
5ml/1 teaspoon bicarbonate of
    soda
10ml/2 teaspoons cream of
    tartar
50g/2oz sugar
2 eggs
150ml/¼ pint milk
25g/1oz softened butter

Sift together the flour, salt, bicarbonate of soda and cream
of tartar, and stir in the sugar. Process the eggs, milk and
butter until smooth (plastic blade). Add the flour mixture
and process until thick and creamy (plastic blade). Cook in
spoonfuls on a hot greased griddle or thick frying pan until
both sides are golden. When cooked, put on a wire rack and
wrap in a clean cloth to keep soft. Serve spread with butter.

Make as above, but use a blender to mix the ingredients until
creamy.

Apple Scones
Add 2 peeled and quartered apples to the milk mixture. Serve
buttered and sprinkled with sugar and cinnamon.

Banana Scones
Put 2 banana slices on each scone when cooking before
turning over. Serve with butter and sugar, or with syrup.

Fluffy Icing

40g/1½oz unsalted butter
15ml/1 tablespoon grated orange or lemon rind
450g/1lb icing sugar
30ml/2 tablespoons orange or lemon juice
15ml/1 tablespoon water

The butter should be soft but not melted. Put into the processor bowl with the rind, and cream until just mixed (plastic blade). Add half the sugar and process until mixed. Add the juice and water and the remaining sugar, and continue processing until light and fluffy.

Make as above, but use a blender.

Gâteau St. Honoré

½ recipe quantity prepared shortcrust pastry (page 122)
1 recipe quantity prepared choux pastry (page 109)

Filling and Topping
300ml/½ pint double cream
60ml/4 tablespoons caster sugar
crystallized violets or roses

Roll out the shortcrust pastry into a 20cm/8in round. Place on a baking sheet and prick well with a fork.

Put the choux pastry into a piping bag fitted with a 1cm/½in plain nozzle. Damp the outside edge of the pastry round and pipe half the choux pastry in adjoining buns round this damp edge. Lightly grease another baking sheet and pipe out the remaining choux pastry in separate buns the same size as the others. Put the choux/shortcrust ring on the top shelf of the oven, and the separate buns on the middle shelf. Bake at 200°C/400°F/Gas Mark 6 for 30 minutes. Cool on a wire rack. Make a small slit in each of the choux buns to allow steam to escape.

Put the cream and 15ml/1 tablespoon sugar into a bowl and whisk to soft peaks. Fill a piping bag and use some of the cream to fill the choux buns. Put the remaining sugar into a small heavy-based saucepan and heat gently until golden and syrupy. Dip the bases of the separate choux buns in this caramel and fix round the top of the choux ring. Trickle any remaining caramel on top of the puffs and decorate at once with crystallized violets or roses. Pipe the remaining cream in the centre of the gâteau and decorate with more violets or roses.

Left Gâteau St Honoré

Glacé Icing

225g/8oz icing sugar
30ml/2 tablespoons hot water
flavourings

Sift the icing sugar into the mixing bowl. Switch on to minimum speed and add the water slowly until the desired consistency is reached. Use the same flavourings as for Butter Icing (page 108).

Make as above, but use the plastic blade.

Hot Water Crust Pastry

350g/12oz plain flour
5ml/1 teaspoon salt
100g/4oz lard
150ml/¼ pint milk and water
mixed

Put the flour and salt into the mixer bowl. Heat the lard and liquid together in a pan until the fat melts. Bring to the boil. Add to the flour in the bowl, and mix on low speed to make a soft dough. Turn on to a lightly floured surface and knead until smooth and free from cracks. Use while warm to make savoury raised pies. This pastry becomes stiff and difficult to handle as it cools. To keep it warm, wrap in polythene and keep in a warm place.

Make as above, but pour the hot lard and liquid through the feeder tube, with the machine running, and process with the plastic blade until a soft dough is formed.

Lemon Yoghurt Cake

3 eggs, separated
175g/6oz plain flour
10ml/2 teaspoons bicarbonate
   of soda
2·5ml/½ teaspoon salt
50g/2oz soft margarine
275g/10oz caster sugar
150ml/¼ pint natural yoghurt
grated rind of 1 lemon

Icing
100g/4oz icing sugar
30ml/2 tablespoons lemon
   juice
grated rind of 1 lemon

Whisk the egg whites to soft peaks and put into a separate bowl. Put the flour, soda, salt, margarine, sugar, egg yolks, yoghurt and lemon rind into the mixer bowl and mix until well blended. Fold in the egg whites. Put the mixture into a greased and floured 20cm/8in cake tin and bake at 180°C/350°F/Gas Mark 4 for 1¼ hours. Turn out and cool on a wire rack.

When the cake is cold, stir together the icing sugar, lemon juice and rind and spread over the cake. Leave for 24 hours before cutting.

Make as above, but mix the flour, soda, salt, margarine, sugar, egg yolks, yoghurt and lemon rind with the plastic blade.

Madeira Cake

250g/9oz plain flour
1 teaspoon baking powder
a pinch of salt
175g/6oz caster sugar
175g/6oz butter
3 eggs
5ml/1 teaspoon grated lemon
    rind
a little milk
1 slice candied citron peel

Sift the flour with the baking powder and salt. Put the sugar and butter into a mixing bowl and beat on low speed until light and fluffy. Add the eggs one at a time, continuing to beat until very light and fluffy. Put in flour mixture and grated lemon rind and switch off mixer as soon as the flour is incorporated, adding a little milk if necessary. The mixture should shake easily from a spoon. Put into a greased and lined 18cm/7in cake tin and bake at 180°C/350°F/Gas Mark 4 for 1 hour 20 minutes. Put the slice of peel on the cake after it has been 30 minutes in the oven.

Make as above, but cream the sugar and butter with the plastic blade. Add the eggs, one at a time, through the feeder tube with the machine running. Add the flour, baking powder and salt with the grated lemon rind and milk, and process just long enough to incorporate the flour.

Flavourings

Cherry
Omit the lemon rind and peel. Add a few drops of vanilla or almond essence to the butter and sugar, and 100g/4oz halved glacé cherries tossed in the flour.

Coconut
Omit lemon rind and peel. Add a few drops of vanilla essence to the butter and sugar. Reduce the flour to 200g/7oz and add 75g/3oz desiccated coconut.

Meringues

3 egg whites
175g/6oz caster sugar

Line a baking sheet with a piece of non-stick vegetable parchment. Put the egg whites into the mixing bowl and whisk until they stand in stiff peaks. Add half the sugar and continue whisking until the mixture is stiff and shiny. Fold in the remaining sugar with a metal spoon. Spoon out the mixture, or pipe it into 16 rounded heaps on the lined baking sheet. Bake at 120°C/250°F/Gas Mark $\frac{1}{2}$ for 2 hours. Turn off the oven but leave in the meringues until the oven is cold. Remove from the baking sheet and store in an airtight tin or

(CONTINUES)

the freezer until required. To serve, sandwich the halves together with whipped cream or ice cream.

If the food processor is fitted with a whisk attachment, put the egg whites into the processor bowl. Fit the lid but leave out the pusher from the feeder tube to admit more air. Whisk until stiff when the whisk attachment will leave track marks as it moves. This will take about 45 seconds, and it is best to process in 15-second stages. With the motor running, pour half the sugar through the feeder tube and process for 20 seconds. Fold in the sugar as above.

Mincemeat Doughnuts

15g/½oz fresh yeast
5ml/1 teaspoon sugar
150ml/¼ pint cider
25g/1oz block margarine
225g/8oz strong plain flour
a pinch of salt
30ml/2 tablespoons fruit
    mincemeat
fat or oil for deep frying
100g/4oz caster sugar
2·5ml/½ teaspoon ground
    cinnamon

Cream the yeast with the sugar. Heat the cider to lukewarm and add the yeast. Leave in a warm place for 10 minutes until the liquid is frothy. Cut the margarine into pieces. Mix the flour, salt and margarine just long enough to break up the margarine and mix with the flour (plastic blade). With the machine running, pour the yeast liquid through the feeder tube and mix to a soft dough. Shape the dough into a ball. Leave the dough in a greased polythene bag in a warm place for about 45 minutes until it has doubled in size. Divide the dough into 12 pieces and knead each one lightly into a ball. Make a deep hole in each and put ½ teaspoon mincemeat in each hole. Mould the dough round so that the mincemeat is covered. Put the dough balls on a greased baking sheet and return the polythene bag. Leave in a warm place for 15 minutes. Remove from the bag. Fry the doughnuts in hot deep fat or oil for 10 minutes, turning occasionally until golden-brown. Drain on kitchen paper. Mix the sugar and cinnamon, and roll the hot doughnuts in this mixture until completely coated. Eat while fresh.

Make as above, but mix and knead the dough with the dough hook of a mixer.

Mocha Fudge Icing

175g/6oz plain chocolate
40g/1½oz soft butter
1 egg
5ml/1 teaspoon vanilla
    essence
75g/3oz icing sugar
150ml/¼ pint hot strong coffee

Cut the chocolate in pieces and chop finely in the blender. Put all the ingredients into the blender except the coffee. Blend for 5 seconds. Remove cover and pour in hot coffee. Blend for 15 seconds. This gives a very creamy texture, but more icing sugar can be added slowly to give a firmer icing if preferred.

Make as above, but chop the chocolate with the metal blade. Process all the ingredients with the metal blade until creamy.

Orange Rock Cakes

75g/3oz butter
75g/3oz caster sugar
1 egg
1 orange
225g/8oz plain flour
10ml/2 teaspoons baking
    powder
25g/1oz chopped mixed peel

Cream the butter and sugar in the mixer until light and fluffy. Add the egg and the grated rind and juice of the orange together with the flour sifted with baking powder. When mixed to a soft dough, stir in the peel. Place in small heaps on greased baking tins and bake at 200°C/400°F/Gas Mark 6 for 15 minutes. Cool on a wire rack.

Make as above, but cream the butter and sugar with the plastic blade. Add the egg, orange rind and juice, flour and baking powder and mix to a soft dough before stirring in the peel.

Potato Pancakes

450g/1lb potatoes
1 small onion
2 eggs
50g/2oz plain flour
5ml/1 teaspoon salt
1·25ml/¼ teaspoon baking
    powder

Cut the potatoes into small pieces and dry them well with kitchen paper. Cut the onion in pieces. Put all the ingredients into the blender and blend until finely chopped. Stop the motor and scrape down the potatoes with a spatula if necessary. Pour this batter on to a hot greased griddle or thick frying pan and brown on each side. These pancakes are very good served hot with butter. They can also be used as an accompaniment to bacon or sausages.

Make as above, but chop the potatoes and onion coarsely with the metal blade. Add the remaining ingredients and process until the potatoes and onion are finely chopped.

Quick Flaky Pastry

225g/8oz plain flour
a pinch of salt
150g/5oz block margarine,
    well chilled
100ml/4fl oz cold water,
    well chilled

Put the flour and salt into the processor bowl. Cut the
margarine into four pieces and put one piece into the bowl.
Process until the mixture is like fine breadcrumbs (plastic
blade). With the machine running, add the water gradually
through the feeder tube until a ball of dough forms. With a
knife, divide the ball of dough into four pieces while still in
the bowl. Cut the remaining margarine into tiny pieces and
sprinkle between the sections of dough. Process just long
enough to mix in the margarine. Put on to a well-floured
board and roll out 5mm/¼in thick. Fold over the top and
bottom of the dough and half turn to the right. Roll out and
fold again, and half turn to the right. Roll out and fold again,
half turn to the right. Roll out once more and fold. Cover and
chill for 30 minutes, then roll out and use.

Make as above, but use a mixer. Mix in the first piece of fat
until the mixture is like fine breadcrumbs. Add the remaining fat in small pieces and only mix just long enough to
amalgamate.

Rich Fruit Buns

7g/¼oz fresh yeast
25g/1oz caster sugar
75ml/5 tablespoons milk
225g/8oz strong plain flour
a pinch of salt
a pinch of ground mixed spice
25g/1oz butter
1 egg
75g/3oz mixed dried fruit

Glaze
25g/1oz sugar
60ml/4 tablespoons water

Cream the yeast with 1 teaspoon of the sugar. Heat the milk
to lukewarm and add the yeast. Leave in a warm place for
10 minutes until the liquid is frothy. Put the flour, salt,
spice and remaining sugar into the processor bowl. Cut the
butter into pieces and add to the bowl. Process until just
mixed (plastic blade). With the machine running, pour the
liquid through the feeder tube and process to a soft dough.
Add the egg and process until just mixed. Stir in the dried
fruit. Shape the dough into a ball. Leave the dough in a
greased polythene bag in a warm place for about 1 hour
until it has doubled in size. Divide into 10 pieces and knead
each one lightly into a ball. Grease a baking sheet, place the
dough balls on it and return to the oiled bag. Leave in a
warm place to prove for 15 minutes. Remove the bag and
bake buns at 220°C/425°F/Gas Mark 7 for 15 minutes. Put
on to a wire rack.

  For the glaze, put the sugar and water into a small pan, stir
until dissolved and boil for 3 minutes. Brush the glaze on to
the hot buns.

(CONTINUES)

Make as above, but mix and knead the dough with the dough hook of a mixer.

Rough Puff Pastry

175g/6oz plain flour
a pinch of salt
150g/5oz butter
45ml/3 tablespoons cold
   water, well chilled

Sift the flour and salt into a mixing bowl, and add the butter cut into 2·5cm/1in pieces. Mix on minimum speed for 30 seconds. Sprinkle with water and turn off mixer as soon as the dough forms. Chill in the refrigerator for 10 minutes. Roll out on a lightly floured board into a rectangle. Fold in three, give the pastry one half turn and roll out again. Fold and leave in the refrigerator for 15 minutes. Repeat the rolling out and resting process twice more, and then roll out to use.

Make as above, but use the plastic blade. Only process long enough for the dough to form.

Royal Icing

450g/1lb icing sugar
2 egg whites
15ml/1 tablespoon lemon
   juice
15ml/1 tablespoon glycerine

Sift the icing sugar. Put the egg whites, lemon juice and glycerine into the mixing bowl and switch on minimum speed, using the heavy beater. Tip in a little sugar at a time, beating until smooth. Continue adding sugar until the mixture is dull-looking and very white, and forms peaks.

Make as above, but use the plastic blade, adding the sugar in small quantities.

Scones

225g/8oz self-raising flour
a pinch of salt
50g/2oz block margarine
25g/1oz caster sugar
90ml/6 tablespoons milk

Put the flour and salt into the mixer bowl. Add the margarine, cut up into small pieces, and mix with the heavy beater until the mixture is like fine breadcrumbs. Add the sugar, then add 75ml/5 tablespoons milk gradually, with the machine running, until a soft dough is formed. Knead the dough lightly on a floured surface for 1 minute. Roll out 2·5cm/1in thick, then cut out 12 rounds using a 5cm/2in cutter. Put the rounds on a greased baking sheet so that they just touch

(CONTINUES)

each other. Brush the tops with the remaining milk. Bake at 220°C/425°F/Gas Mark 7 for 12 minutes. Cool on a wire rack.

Make as above, but process the flour, salt and margarine with the plastic blade. Add the milk gradually through the feeder tube with the machine running to form a soft dough.

Cheese Scones
Omit the sugar. Add 50g/2oz grated or chopped Cheddar cheese with the milk.

Cheese and Onion Scones
Add 1 finely chopped small onion with the cheese and milk. A pinch of dried mixed herbs may also be added.

Fruit Scones
Stir in 50g/2oz mixed dried fruit before rolling out.

Shortcrust Pastry

225g/8oz plain flour
a pinch of salt
50g/2oz lard
50g/2oz block margarine
45ml/3 tablespoons cold water

Put the flour and salt into the processor bowl. Cut the lard and margarine into cubes and add to the flour. Process until the mixture is like fine breadcrumbs (plastic blade). With the machine switched on, add water through the feeder tube to make a firm dough. Roll out and use as required.

Make as above, but use the heavy beater of the mixer to amalgamate the flour and fat, first at minimum speed, then at Speed 2 as the fat breaks up. When the mixture looks like fine breadcrumbs, add the water quickly and switch off as soon as it is incorporated.

Wholemeal Pastry
Substitute plain wholemeal flour for white flour. It may be necessary to scrape down the bowl once or twice during processing as wholemeal flour tends to fly about the bowl. Add a little more water if necessary as wholemeal flour is a little more absorbent than white.

Savoury Pastry
Add 50g/2oz grated Cheddar cheese to the flour. Season with a pinch of pepper and a pinch of mustard powder.

Simple Gingerbread

225g/8oz plain flour
50g/2oz dark soft brown
    sugar
10ml/2 teaspoons ground
    ginger
5ml/1 teaspoon ground mixed
    spice
5ml/1 teaspoon bicarbonate of
    soda
2 eggs
150ml/$\frac{1}{4}$ pint milk
175g/6oz black treacle
50g/2oz golden syrup
100g/4oz margarine

Put the flour, sugar, ginger, spice and soda into the processor bowl and add the eggs and milk. Mix until just blended (plastic blade). Put the treacle, syrup and margarine into a pan and warm together until the margarine has melted. Cool until lukewarm. With the machine running, pour the treacle mixture through the feeder tube and mix until just blended. Put the mixture into a greased and lined 18cm/7in square tin. Bake at 150°C/300°F/Gas Mark 2 for 1$\frac{1}{2}$ hours. Cool in the tin for 10 minutes and then turn out on a wire rack to cool. Gingerbread tastes better if stored in a tin for a day or two before cutting.

Make as above, but mix the flour, sugar, ginger, spice and soda with the eggs and milk in a mixer until just blended. Add the warm syrup mixture with the machine running and mix until just blended.

Suet Pastry

225g/8oz self-raising flour
5ml/1 teaspoon salt
100g/4oz shredded suet
150ml/$\frac{1}{4}$ pint cold water

Put the flour, salt and suet into the processor bowl. With the machine running, pour the water through the feeder tube until the dough forms (plastic blade). The pastry should be soft but not sticky, so add the water slowly – you may not need it all. Knead lightly on a floured board and roll out or form into dumplings. This pastry may be boiled, steamed or baked.

Make as above, but mix the flour, salt and suet with a mixer before adding the water gradually.

Surprise Muffins

225g/8oz self-raising flour
2·5ml/½ teaspoon salt
2·5ml/½ teaspoon mustard
    powder
pepper
100g/4oz butter or margarine
50g/2oz Cheddar cheese
50g/2oz seedless raisins
1 egg
150ml/¼ pint milk

Sift the flour, salt, mustard powder and pepper into a mixing bowl. Cut the fat into small pieces and, with the mixer on low speed, work the fat into the flour, until the mixture is like breadcrumbs. Stir in the grated cheese and the raisins, and then add the egg and milk. Mix on low speed to a soft dough. Grease some deep bun tins and put in the mixture (this quantity should make 18-20 muffins). Bake at 200°C/400°F/Gas Mark 6 for 20 minutes. Split open while still warm and spread with butter, serving immediately.

Make as above, but use the plastic blade. The cheese may be prepared first with a grating disc, or finely chopped with the metal blade.

Sweet Biscuits

100g/4oz block margarine
150g/5oz caster sugar
1 egg yolk
225g/8oz plain flour
flavouring

Cut the margarine into small pieces. Mix all the ingredients, except flavouring, to a firm dough (plastic blade). Add the chosen flavouring (see below), and process until just mixed. Grease an 18 × 28cm/7 × 11in tin and press the mixture into it. Bake at 180°C/350°F/Gas Mark 4 for 30 minutes. Cool and cut into squares.

Make as above, but use a mixer to cream the margarine and sugar before adding the egg yolk, flour and flavouring.

Almond Biscuits
Add 5ml/1 teaspoon almond essence and 25g/1oz flaked almonds. Press into the tin and sprinkle with 25g/1oz flaked almonds before baking.

Coconut Biscuits
Use 175g/6oz plain flour and 50g/2oz desiccated coconut with 50g/2oz chopped glacé cherries.

Ginger Biscuits
Add 5ml/1 teaspoon ground ginger and 25g/1oz chopped crystallized ginger.

Sweet Flan Pastry

100g/4oz butter
5ml/1 teaspoon caster sugar
a pinch of salt
175g/6oz plain flour
1 egg yolk
10ml/2 teaspoons cold water

Put the butter, sugar and salt into the mixer bowl, switch to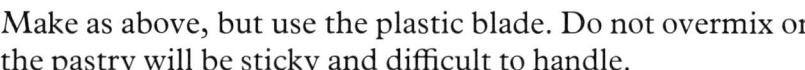
minimum speed, tip in the flour and gradually increase the
speed as the fat breaks up. Mix until the mixture looks like
fine breadcrumbs. Stir the egg yolk and water together, add
to the mixture, and switch off as soon as the liquid is mixed
in. Roll out carefully as this pastry is very fragile. Use for
sweet flans.

Make as above, but use the plastic blade. Do not overmix or
the pastry will be sticky and difficult to handle.

Truffle Cakes

225g/8oz any stale cake
25g/1oz cocoa
15ml/1 tablespoon rum or
  brandy
150ml/¼ pint syrup from
  canned fruit or diluted
  orange squash
60ml/4 tablespoons apricot
  jam
45ml/3 tablespoons water
100g/4oz chocolate vermicelli
a little icing sugar

Break the cake into pieces and make into crumbs (metal
blade). Change to the plastic blade and add the cocoa and
rum or brandy. With the machine running, add the syrup or
squash slowly through the feeder tube (plastic blade). The
mixture should be firm enough to roll easily in the hands, so
check the consistency before adding all the liquid, and omit
a little if necessary. Roll the mixture with the hands into 12
balls. Leave in the refrigerator for 1 hour. Put the apricot
jam and water into a small pan and heat together until the
jam has melted. Put the chocolate vermicelli on a plate.
Using tongs or 2 soup spoons, dip the truffle balls quickly
into the jam and roll in the vermicelli. Put into paper cake
cases. Leave for 1 hour until firm and sprinkle the tops lightly
with a little sifted icing sugar.

Make as above, but use the blender to make cake crumbs.
Remove to a bowl and work in the remaining ingredients
with a mixer or by hand.

An assortment of wholemeal breads and rolls

Wholemeal Bread

1·4kg/3lb wholemeal flour
900ml/1½ pints warm water
40g/1½oz fresh yeast
25g/1oz salt
25g/1oz sugar

Use half the flour to make a batter with all the water. Blend the yeast with 30ml/2 extra tablespoons warm water and stir into the batter. Leave to stand for 15 minutes, covered with a damp cloth. Add the remaining flour, salt and sugar, and mix with dough hook on lowest speed for 3 minutes. Divide dough between greased loaf tins (this amount will fit 4 × 450g/1lb loaf tins) and leave to stand in a warm place for 1 hour until the dough doubles in size. Bake at 230°C/450°F/Gas Mark 8 for 45 minutes, turning loaves half-way through cooking time, moving them through a right angle in the oven. Cool on a wire tray.

Make as above, but mix the dough with the plastic blade.

Spreads, Pastes and Dips

Anchovy Spread

12 anchovy fillets
30ml/2 tablespoons
    mayonnaise
45ml/3 tablespoons double
    cream
1 slice of onion
1·25ml/$\frac{1}{4}$ teaspoon mustard
    powder
175g/6oz full-fat soft cheese

Drain the oil from the anchovy fillets. Rinse the fillets in a little water and pat dry with kitchen paper. Put into the blender with the mayonnaise, cream, onion and mustard powder. Cover and blend for 10 seconds. Cut up the cheese into small cubes. With the motor running, drop the cheese through opening in lid, and continue blending until smooth. It may be necessary to stop the motor once or twice and push down the mixture with a spatula to ensure smooth blending. Use this spread on cocktail biscuits or squares of toast, or as a filling for small sandwiches.

Make as above, but use the metal blade.

Aubergine Caviar

2 aubergines
2 thin-skinned lemons
2 garlic cloves
100ml/4fl oz salad oil
2·5ml/$\frac{1}{2}$ teaspoon salt

Trim the stem and base from each aubergine. Split them through lengthways and place cut-side down on an ungreased baking sheet. Bake at 200°C/400°C/Gas Mark 6 for 45 minutes. Cool completely and then scrape the flesh out of the skins. Cut the lemons in quarters and discard the pips. Cut each piece of lemon in half and half again. Chop the lemon pieces (including skin) very finely (metal blade). Skin the garlic and add to the processor with the aubergine flesh, oil and salt, and continue mixing until smooth. Put into a serving bowl and chill for 2 hours before serving with pieces of raw vegetables or salted cocktail biscuits.

Make as above, but use a blender to chop the lemons and mix the aubergines and other ingredients.

Avocado Dip

1 lemon
1 large ripe avocado
60ml/4 tablespoons salad oil
2 garlic cloves
1 small onion
salt and pepper

Peel the lemon and remove the pips. Cut in pieces and blend until very finely chopped. Cut the avocado in half and spoon the flesh into the blender. Add the oil, garlic and coarsely chopped onion in the blender with the salt and pepper. Blend until smooth, and chill. This is very good served with pieces of cucumber and celery, and with crisps.

Make as above, but chop the lemon with the metal blade. Process all the ingredients until smooth, using the metal blade.

Blue Cheese Dip

1 small carrot
1 onion
225g/8oz cottage cheese
100g/4oz Danish Blue
    cheese
45ml/3 tablespoons soured
    cream
3 sprigs parsley
1 garlic clove
salt and pepper
4 drops Tabasco sauce

Peel the carrot and onion and cut into pieces. Chop finely (metal blade). Add the cottage cheese and the Danish Blue cheese broken into small pieces, and process. Add the soured cream, parsley, garlic, salt, pepper and Tabasco sauce. Continue mixing until smooth. Adjust seasoning and put into a serving bowl. Chill for an hour before serving.

Make as above, but chop the vegetables in a blender. Process the cheeses and other ingredients also in a blender.

Chicken and Ham Spread

175g/6oz cooked chicken
100g/4oz cooked ham
1 small onion
1 celery stick
60ml/4 tablespoons
    mayonnaise
30ml/2 tablespoons sweet
    chutney
2·5ml/½ teaspoon vinegar
salt and pepper
2 hard-boiled eggs

Cut the chicken and ham into small pieces, being sure to include the ham fat. Skin the onion and cut into small pieces. Wash, trim and cut the celery. Chop the chicken, ham, onion and celery finely (metal blade). Add the mayonnaise, chutney, vinegar, salt and pepper and continue processing until smooth. Cut the eggs into pieces and add to the mixture. Process until the eggs are finely chopped. Put into a serving dish and chill. Use with toast or in sandwiches.

Make as above, but chop the chicken, ham, onion and celery separately in a blender. Put all the ingredients except the eggs into the blender and process until smooth. Add the eggs and blend until finely chopped.

Devilled Ham

100g/4oz cooked ham
3 hard-boiled eggs
1 small onion
25g/1oz chutney
15ml/1 tablespoon
   mayonnaise
½ teaspoon curry powder

Cut the ham, eggs and onion into pieces. Put into the blender and add the chutney, mayonnaise and curry powder. Blend to the required smoothness. The mixture may be creamy, but a slightly rough texture is often more attractive, particularly if spread on toast.

Make as above, but chop the ham, eggs and onion finely with the metal blade. Add the remaining ingredients and continue processing with the metal blade until smooth.

Flavoured Butters

Flavoured butters are useful as spreads for bread or pancakes, as a base for sandwiches, and as dressings for meat and fish. The butter should be at room temperature, and blended at low speed until smooth, stopping the machine to scrape down if necessary. Additions such as nuts or herbs should be made only when the butter is well creamed, and the blender should then be run on high speed just until the additions are coarsely chopped.

Make as above, but use the metal blade to blend and chop the ingredients.

Garlic Butter
Add 1 garlic clove and a pinch of salt to 100g/4oz butter. Use for rolls, French bread or grilled meat.

Honey Butter
Add 60ml/4 tablespoons liquid honey and a pinch of salt to 100g/4oz butter. Use for toast or biscuits.

Maple Butter
Add 60ml/4 tablespoons maple syrup, 30ml/2 tablespoons liquid honey and 50g/2oz walnuts to 100g/4oz butter. Use for pancakes or waffles.

Parsley Butter
Add 6 sprigs parsley and a squeeze of lemon juice to 100g/4oz butter. Use for grilled meat or fish.

(CONTINUES)

Watercress Butter
Add $\frac{1}{2}$ bunch washed and dried watercress, pinch of salt, 15ml/1 tablespoon lemon juice and a pinch of celery seed to 100g/4oz butter. Use for grilled meat or fish.

Horseradish Dip

60ml/4 tablespoons soured
  cream
1 small onion
1·25ml/$\frac{1}{4}$ teaspoon salt
25g/1oz grated horseradish
2 drops Worcestershire sauce
225g/8oz full-fat soft cheese

Put the sour cream, coarsely chopped onion, salt, horseradish and Worcestershire sauce into the blender. Blend until the onion is finely chopped. Cut the cream cheese into small pieces and add to the blender slowly. Blend until smooth, and chill before using. This is good served with small hot cocktail sausages.

Make as above, but chop the onion coarsely with the metal blade. Add all the remaining ingredients and process with the metal blade until smooth.

Peanut Butter

225g/8oz salted peanuts
45ml/3 tablespoons salad oil

Chop the peanuts finely (metal blade). Add the oil through the feeder tube, and continue processing until smooth. Store in a screwtop jar. For a very fresh flavour, buy peanuts in the shell, roast them in the oven and then shell them. Use them with their skins on and add salt to taste.

Make as above, but chop the peanuts in a blender and then gradually add the oil through the lid.

Crunchy Peanut Butter
Chop peanuts coarsely (metal blade). Remove one-third of the nuts and keep on one side. Continue chopping until the nuts are very fine, then add oil and process until smooth. Stir in the remaining nuts before putting into a storage jar.

Peanut Honey Butter
Process basic peanut butter, adding 30ml/2 tablespoons of clear honey.

Prawn Dip

225g/8oz shelled prawns
100g/4oz crabmeat
225g/8oz full-fat soft cheese
150ml/¼ pint natural yoghurt
15ml/1 tablespoon tomato
   ketchup
15ml/1 tablespoon lemon
   juice
salt and pepper

Chop the prawns coarsely (metal blade). Keep on one side. Put all the other ingredients into the bowl and mix thoroughly until smooth and creamy (plastic blade). Add to the prawns and stir just enough to distribute the prawns. Chill for an hour before serving with small salted biscuits.

Make as above, but chop the prawns coarsely in a blender and remove to a bowl. Blend the other ingredients until smooth and then stir in the prawns.

Soft Cheese Dips

175g/6oz full-fat soft cheese
45ml/3 tablespoons single
   cream
salt and pepper

Cut the cheese into small pieces. Mix with the cream, salt and pepper to a soft dipping consistency (plastic blade). This makes the basic dip which can then be flavoured (see below). Add flavouring ingredients and chop them finely into the dip mixture (metal blade). Serve with small cocktail biscuits, crisps or pieces of raw vegetables.

Make as above, but use a blender to mix the dip.

Autumn Dip
Add 1 red-skinned eating apple (with peel on), 2 celery sticks, 50g/2oz walnut halves.

Devil Dip
Add 2 hard-boiled eggs, 1 small onion, 30ml/2 tablespoons mustard pickle, 30ml/2 tablespoons vinegar, 5ml/1 teaspoon curry powder.

Horseradish Dip
Add 1 small onion, 30ml/2 tablespoons horseradish cream, 2 rashers grilled lean bacon, 15ml/1 tablespoon mayonnaise.

Salad Dip
Add 1 small green pepper, 3 spring onions, ½ unpeeled cucumber, 1 garlic clove, sprig of parsley, sprig of thyme.

Preserves and Pickles

All jars for preserving should be sterilized with boiling water and thoroughly dried and kept slightly warm in a very low oven, so that the hot mixture can be poured into them without damage. Jams should be covered with a waxed disc and cellophane or a screwtop or firm plastic top. Vinegar-based pickles must be secured by a firm plastic lid, or by a screwtop lined with a vinegar-proof disc. Paper alone is not good enough for pickles as they will dry out. Jars are best stored in a cool, dry, dark place.

Apple Butter

450g/1lb cooking apples
150ml/¼ pint water
225g/8oz caster sugar
5ml/1 teaspoon ground cinnamon
1·25ml/¼ teaspoon ground allspice
2·5ml/½ teaspoon ground nutmeg
1·25ml/¼ teaspoon ground cloves
a pinch of salt
1 thin slice lemon

Use apples which become fluffy when cooked. Cut the apples into quarters, but do not peel them. Remove the cores, and then cut the flesh into pieces. Put all the ingredients into the blender and blend until the apples are finely chopped. Cook gently for 45 minutes, stirring occasionally, and pour into hot jars. The same recipe can be used for plums or damsons. This makes a good filling for tarts, but fruit butters used to be stored in wide-topped jars. They were then turned out, cut into slices, and served with cream.

Make as above, but chop the apples finely with the metal blade.

Blackcurrant Jam

900g/2lb blackcurrants
15g/½oz butter
300ml/½ pint water
1·4kg/3lb sugar

Remove stems from the blackcurrants and rinse the fruit well. Put the blackcurrants into the blender and blend until well broken up. Put into a greased pan. Rinse the blender with the water, and add the liquid to the pan. Bring the fruit to the boil and stir well until any fruit skins are soft. Add the sugar and stir over low heat until the sugar has dissolved. Boil rapidly for about 5 minutes until setting point is reached. Pour into warm jars and cover.

Make as above, but chop the blackcurrants coarsely with the metal blade.

Golden Jam

1·4kg/3lb cooking apples
1·4kg/3lb eating pears
1·2 litres/2 pints dry cider
1·8kg/4lb sugar
1·25ml/¼ teaspoon ground
    ginger

Peel and core the apples and pears and tie the peel and cores in a large piece of muslin. Chop the flesh coarsely (metal blade). Put the flesh into a preserving pan with the cider and the muslin bag and simmer for 40 minutes. The fruit should be soft but with some pieces still whole. Take out the muslin bag and squeeze thoroughly to return all the juice to the pan. Stir in the sugar and heat gently, stirring until the sugar has dissolved. Add the ginger and bring to the boil. Boil rapidly until setting point is reached. Pour into warm jars and cover.

Make as above, but chop the apples and pears with a little cider in a blender, processing a small quantity at a time.

Gooseberry Jam

900g/2lb gooseberries
300ml/½ pint water
15g/½oz butter
1·4kg/3lb sugar

Top and tail the gooseberries and rinse them well. Put the gooseberries into the blender with the water and blend until well chopped. Put into a greased pan, bring to the boil, and simmer until the fruit skins are soft. Add the sugar and stir over low heat until dissolved. Bring to the boil and boil rapidly for about 5 minutes until setting point is reached. Pour into warm jars and cover.

Make as above, but chop the gooseberries without water, using the metal blade.

Rhubarb Conserve

1·8kg/4lb rhubarb
1·8kg/4lb sugar
1 lemon
50g/2oz blanched split
    almonds

Wipe the rhubarb and cut it into pieces. Put into the blender and blend until coarsely chopped. Put into a saucepan over low heat until the juice runs. Add the sugar, grated rind and juice of the lemon, and split almonds. Stir until the sugar has dissolved, and then boil for 45 minutes until thick and brown. Pour into warm jars and cover.

Make as above, but chop the rhubarb coarsely with the metal blade.

Old Fashioned Mincemeat

175g/6oz cooking apples
225g/8oz seedless raisins
225g/8oz sultanas
225g/8oz currants
100g/4oz mixed candied peel
50g/2oz blanched almonds
100g/4oz shredded suet
225g/8oz dark soft brown
   sugar
1 lemon
2.5ml/½ teaspoon ground
   mixed spice
2.5ml/½ teaspoon ground
   cinnamon

Peel and core the apples and chop them finely (metal blade). Tip into a mixing bowl. Chop raisins, sultanas and currants coarsely (metal blade). Be very careful when chopping the fruit as the machine works very quickly and the fruit should be chopped and not made into a paste. Tip into the bowl with the apples. If the peel is not already chopped, chop it coarsely (metal blade). Chop the almonds coarsely (metal blade). Add to the other fruit with the suet and sugar. Grate the rind from the lemon and squeeze out the juice. Add the rind, juice and spices to the mincemeat. Mix thoroughly, and pack into sterilized jars. Cover and store in a cool dry place.

Make as above, but chop the apples finely in a blender. Chop the dried fruit in small quantities, watching carefully so that the blender does not make a purée. Chop the almonds coarsely in a blender.

Chunky Marmalade

1.4kg/3lb Seville oranges
2 lemons
3.6 litres/6 pints water
2.7kg/6lb sugar

Scrub the oranges and lemons and cut them into small pieces, being sure to save any juice. Remove the pips and tie them in a muslin bag. Chop the fruit coarsely (metal blade). Put into a preserving pan with any juice which has run out. Add the water and the bag of pips. Bring to the boil and then simmer for about 1½ hours until the peel is soft and the quantity of mixture reduced to a half. Remove the bag of pips and squeeze out liquid into the pan. Stir in the sugar and heat gently until it has dissolved. Boil rapidly for about 20 minutes until setting point is reached. Remove from the heat at once and leave to stand for 15 minutes. Skim with a perforated spoon, and then stir thoroughly to distribute the peel. Pour into warm jars and cover.

Make as above, but chop the fruit coarsely in small quantities in a blender, and add a little of the water to make chopping easier.

Left Chunky Marmalade and an assortment of jams

Jelly Marmalade

8 Seville oranges
2 sweet oranges
4·8 litres/8 pints water
3·2kg/7lb sugar
2 lemons

Cut the oranges into four pieces without peeling. Remove the pips, and tie them in a muslin bag. Put some of the oranges and some of the water into the blender, and blend until the oranges are just chopped. Put into the pan with the bag of pips. Continue blending the oranges and water until all the oranges are used up. Add the remaining water, and leave to stand overnight. Boil for 30 minutes and strain through muslin or a jelly bag. Add the sugar together with the juice of the lemons. Heat gently and stir until the sugar has dissolved. Boil rapidly until setting point is reached. Remove any scum, pour the jelly into warm jars, and cover. Skim with a perforated spoon.

Make as above, but chop the oranges without water, using the metal blade.

Three Fruit Marmalade

2 sweet oranges
4 lemons
2 grapefruit
3·6 litres/6 pints water
2·7kg/6lb sugar

Scrub the oranges and lemons, cut them into small pieces and remove the pips. Peel the grapefruit and scrape off all the white pith from the skin and from the fruit. Cut the fruit and peel into pieces, and remove the pips. Tie all the pips in a small muslin bag. Chop the fruit and peel coarsely (metal blade). Put all the fruit and peel into a preserving pan with any juice which has run out and add the water and the bag of pips. Bring to the boil and then simmer for about 1½ hours until the peel is soft and the quantity of mixture reduced to a half. Take out the bag of pips and squeeze any liquid into the pan. Stir in the sugar over low heat until dissolved and then boil rapidly for about 20 minutes until setting point is reached. Remove from the heat at once and leave to stand for 15 minutes. Skim with a perforated spoon, and then stir thoroughly to distribute the peel. Pour into warm jars and cover.

Make as above, but chop the fruit coarsely in small quantities in a blender, and add a little of the water to make chopping easier.

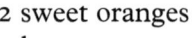

Apple Mint Chutney

900g/2lb cooking apples
900g/2lb onions
450g/1lb red tomatoes
8 tablespoons mint leaves
3 large sprigs parsley
225g/8oz sultanas
2 lemons
450g/1lb dark soft brown
    sugar
600ml/1 pint white vinegar
10ml/2 teaspoons salt
10ml/2 teaspoons ground
    mixed spice

Peel and core the apples and cut them in quarters. Skin the
onions and cut them into large pieces. Chop the apples and
onions (metal blade). Skin the tomatoes by dipping them
into boiling water. Chop the tomatoes (metal blade) and
chop the mint and parsley (metal blade). Put the apples,
onions, tomatoes and herbs into a large preserving pan. Add
the sultanas. Grate the rind from the lemons and extract the
juice. Add the rind and juice to the pan with the sugar,
vinegar, salt and spices. Stir over low heat until the sugar has
dissolved. Bring to the boil, then simmer gently, stirring
occasionally, for about $1\frac{1}{2}$ hours until the chutney is thick
and brown. Pour into warm jars and seal.

Make as above, but chop the apples, onions, tomatoes and
herbs in a blender in small quantities. Add a little of the
vinegar to make chopping easier.

Cranberry Relish

450g/1lb cranberries
1 orange
75ml/3fl oz boiling water
100g/4oz seedless raisins
675g/1$\frac{1}{2}$lb sugar
225g/8oz walnuts

Put the cranberries into 150ml/$\frac{1}{4}$ pint cold water and boil
until the skins break. Put into blender, cover, and blend for
5 seconds. Peel the orange and cut the flesh in small pieces.
Add to the blender, cover and blend for 5 seconds. Add the
cranberry and orange mixture to the boiling water, raisins
and sugar. Bring to the boil and simmer for 20 minutes. Put
the walnuts in the blender, cover, and chop coarsely. Stir
into the cranberry mixture, cool and fill small jars, then seal.
This can be eaten with turkey, pork or ham, and it is also very
good as a filling for small tarts.

Make as above, but chop the cooked cranberries finely with
the metal blade. Chop the peeled orange finely with the
metal blade. Chop the walnuts coarsely with the metal blade.

Indian Chutney

4 large green peppers
4 large red peppers
12 green tomatoes
3 cucumbers
2 large onions
40g/1½oz salt
225g/8oz white-heart cabbage
100g/4oz sugar
750ml/1¼ pints cider vinegar
40g/1½oz mustard seed
5ml/1 teaspoon turmeric
5ml/1 teaspoon ground
   cinnamon
10ml/2 teaspoons ground
   ginger
2·5ml/½ teaspoon ground mace
3 bay leaves

Remove the stems, membranes and seeds from the peppers. Put the peppers, tomatoes, unpeeled cucumbers and onions through the mincer attachment, using the coarse screen. Stir the salt into the vegetables and leave to stand overnight. Drain the vegetables through a colander, pressing down firmly to force out the brine which will have formed. Shred the cabbage finely with a shredding attachment, or through the fine screen of the mincer. Mix all the vegetables together and heat slowly to simmering point, stirring gently from time to time. Add the remaining ingredients and bring to boiling point. Boil for 3 minutes, and remove the bay leaves. The chutney should be very soft and the liquid should have evaporated. Pour into warm jars and seal.

Make as above, but chop the peppers, tomatoes, cucumbers and onions finely with the metal blade. Shred the cabbage with the shredding disc.

Mixed Mustard Pickles

1 marrow
1 cucumber
450g/1lb French beans
1 cauliflower
450g/1lb pickling onions
25g/1oz cooking salt
275g/10oz sugar
50g/2oz plain flour
50g/2oz mustard powder
15g/½oz turmeric
15g/½oz ground ginger
15g/½oz ground nutmeg
1·2 litres/2 pints vinegar

Wipe but do not peel the marrow. Remove seeds and pith. Chop coarsely (metal blade) and put into a large bowl. Wipe but do not peel the cucumber and chop it (metal blade). Top and tail the French beans and chop (metal blade). Add cucumber and French beans to the marrow. Remove green leaves from the cauliflower, and break the cauliflower up into small pieces. Add to the bowl with the skinned onions. Sprinkle with the salt, cover with cold water and leave overnight. Drain off the water. Mix the sugar, flour, spices and a little of the vinegar to make a smooth paste. Put the vegetables into a pan with the remaining vinegar and simmer until just tender. Add a little of the boiling vinegar to the paste and mix well. Return to the pan and simmer for 10 minutes, stirring well. Put into warm jars and seal.

Make as above, but chop the marrow, cucumber and beans in a blender, adding a little water to make chopping easier.

Right Apple Mint Chutney (page 137)

Pepper and Onion Pickle

8 green peppers
3 large onions
100g/4oz sugar
350ml/12fl oz vinegar
15g/½oz salt

Cut the peppers in quarters and remove the stems, membranes and seeds. Skin the onions and cut them in pieces. Put the peppers and onions into the blender in small quantities with just enough water to cover. Blend until the vegetables are chopped in small pieces. Drain off the water and put the peppers and onions into a bowl. Cover with boiling water and leave for 15 minutes. Drain and cover again with boiling water, and leave for a further 15 minutes. Drain again and put into a large saucepan with the sugar, vinegar and salt. Bring to the boil and simmer for 30 minutes. Pack into hot jars and seal. Use as a pickle, or add a few spoonfuls to winter casseroles or pies when peppers are expensive.

Make as above, but chop the peppers and onions without water, using the metal blade.

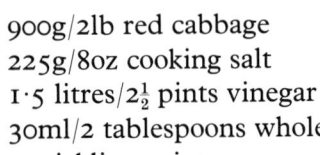

Pickled Red Cabbage

900g/2lb red cabbage
225g/8oz cooking salt
1·5 litres/2½ pints vinegar
30ml/2 tablespoons whole
   pickling spice

Discard the discoloured leaves from the cabbage. Cut the cabbage into 8 wedges and discard the hard core. Shred with the shredding attachment of a mixer. Arrange alternate layers of cabbage and salt in a bowl, cover and leave in a cool place overnight. Put the vinegar and spice into a pan, bring to the boil and then simmer for 15 minutes. Leave until cold and then strain to remove the spices. Drain the salt liquid from the cabbage. Rinse the cabbage in cold water and drain completely. Pack into sterilized jars and pour on the cold vinegar to cover completely. Press down the cabbage with the handle of a wooden spoon from time to time as the vinegar is poured in so that air pockets are eliminated. Cover with vinegar-proof lids. Keep for a week before using, but do not store longer than 3 months, or the cabbage will become very soft.

Make as above, but slice the cabbage with the shredding disc.

900g/2lb stoned plums
450g/1lb carrots
600ml/1 pint vinegar
450g/1lb seedless raisins
450g/1lb soft brown sugar
1 garlic clove
25g/1oz chillies
25g/1oz ground ginger
40g/1½oz salt

Plum Chutney

Put the plums into the blender and blend on low speed until
chopped, and put into a saucepan. Scrape or peel the carrots,
according to age, and cut them into pieces. Put into the
blender with some of the vinegar, and chop finely. Put into
the saucepan with the rest of the vinegar, raisins and sugar.
Crush the garlic clove with a palette knife, and chop the
chillies. Add to the saucepan with the ginger and salt. Bring
to the boil, and simmer until thick and brown, stirring well.
Put into warm jars and seal.

Make as above, but chop the plums and carrots without
vinegar, using the metal blade.

Index

Page references of illustrations are in *italics*. **Bold** type is used for principal ingredients of the recipes.